MOM
 O
GR

MOMENTS *of* GRACE

*Faithfulness
When Life Hurts*

JANAE HOFER

WESTBOW
PRESS®
A DIVISION OF THOMAS NELSON
& ZONDERVAN

Copyright © 2022 Janae Hofer.

All rights reserved. No part of this book may be used or reproduced by any means, graphic, electronic, or mechanical, including photocopying, recording, taping or by any information storage retrieval system without the written permission of the author except in the case of brief quotations embodied in critical articles and reviews.

This book is a work of non-fiction. Unless otherwise noted, the author and the publisher make no explicit guarantees as to the accuracy of the information contained in this book and in some cases, names of people and places have been altered to protect their privacy.

WestBow Press books may be ordered through booksellers or by contacting:

WestBow Press
A Division of Thomas Nelson & Zondervan
1663 Liberty Drive
Bloomington, IN 47403
www.westbowpress.com
844-714-3454

Because of the dynamic nature of the Internet, any web addresses or links contained in this book may have changed since publication and may no longer be valid. The views expressed in this work are solely those of the author and do not necessarily reflect the views of the publisher, and the publisher hereby disclaims any responsibility for them.

Any people depicted in stock imagery provided by Getty Images are models, and such images are being used for illustrative purposes only. Certain stock imagery © Getty Images.

Scriptures taken from the Holy Bible, New International Version®, NIV®. Copyright © 1973, 1978, 1984, 2011 by Biblica, Inc.™ Used by permission of Zondervan. All rights reserved worldwide. www.zondervan.com The "NIV" and "New International Version" are trademarks registered in the United States Patent and Trademark Office by Biblica, Inc.®

Interior Image Credit: Janae Hofer

ISBN: 978-1-6642-7003-9 (sc)
ISBN: 978-1-6642-7004-6 (hc)
ISBN: 978-1-6642-7002-2 (e)

Library of Congress Control Number: 2022911573

Print information available on the last page.

WestBow Press rev. date: 07/19/2022

*To my parents and grandparents,
who taught me the true meaning of grace.*

Introduction

Life is made up of moments—significant and insignificant. These ever-passing moments make up who we are and who we become. Some are blissful, and we wish to stay in their glow forever. Some are painful, and we attempt to dim them from our consciences, only to see the unwelcome flashbacks in dreams. Some are mundane and seemingly inconsequential.

Whether or not we recognize it, these are all moments of grace from our sovereign God. Even if His unfailing compassionate love is not seen by our weary eyes, His grace is ever-present. In 2 Corinthians 12:9, God promises that His grace is sufficient for us. His endless grace is not sufficient only sometimes—it is sufficient all of the time. It is sufficient in moments of joy and sorrow. It is sufficient in moments of unbelievable excitement and mind-numbing boredom. It is even sufficient in the face of loss and confusion.

My life—uniquely marked with physical brokenness—is no exception to this grace. Indeed, my life is woven by the same golden thread that weaves others' lives. This golden thread runs through every moment, steadying in upheaval, guiding in uncertainty, and shining bright in success. This golden thread is God's grace, always present, even when temporarily hidden by the fog of this fallen world.

This book is my story told through my human lens, admittedly cracked, calibrated to God's grace. Although we will not have a full view of God's grace until the longed-for day of eternity, you and I can decisively reflect on the grace God generously gives. This reflective focus will reveal glimpses of the golden thread in all of life's moments. Understanding these glimpses of grace allows us to express our stories with humility and gratitude. Humility recognizes that our successes are only by His grace. Inversely, humility also allows us to express who we truly are without belittling ourselves, even in the midst of failures. Understanding grace also leads to natural expressions of gratitude for how God's grace has preserved, comforted, and guided us.

As the pages of my story reveal, true humility and gratitude can't be generated with disingenuous outward platitudes. Many times, I have been composed on the outside, while inwardly cursing the life that I saw as ruined by the carnage of disability-related hardships. I felt like a burden and hindrance to my family. I struggled to identify genuine friendships. I sometimes angrily fought through the elementary, secondary, postsecondary, and legal education systems, which are understandably inherently averse to individuals with severe physical disabilities. I chafed at my limited career options while simultaneously bemoaning the intelligence that obligated me to strive for gainful employment. I fumed as I began spending thousands of dollars on medical expenses each year, realizing that, even as an associate attorney at a large private law firm, I would be in a better financial position if I remained on disability assistance. Moreover, I angrily longed to escape from the harsh corporate legal world into a more caring and nurturing profession such teaching or nursing, questioning why God gave me a tender, feminine spirit and yet still expected me to work in a "man's world." Most personally, I cringed at trying to find true love in the face of my physical baggage.

I could reiterate all the Christianese sayings:

- "God has a plan."
- "God is a loving and good God."
- "God is gracious and always provides."
- "I couldn't have done this without God."

But until I honestly faced my disappointments with God, doubts about His gracious love, and self-reliant pride in my accomplishments, I couldn't continually abide in His unwavering peace with my past, present, and future circumstances.

It was then that I confronted my disappointments, doubts, and pride, not only by acknowledging their existence but also by moving forward to a place of understanding. One way of gaining understanding is by analyzing life with what I call recalibration questions:

- How do I see God working out His plan in my life?
- Where in my life have I seen God's love and goodness even in the midst of hardships?
- How has He provided for me physically, emotionally, spiritually, relationally, and financially?
- Do I really attribute my successes to God, or do I secretly attribute the credit to my hardworking stamina?
- Where would I be without Him?

These are the soul-searching questions that I pondered for years prior to writing this book. Pondering these questions in contrast to only dwelling on the "why-would-God" or "how-could-God" questions has led me from a place of suicidal depression and prideful anger to a place of gratitude and humility. I couldn't help but arrive at this place in light of identifying the golden thread of God's grace weaving through even the most painful and unpleasant moments of my life.

My parents often said that life is "90 percent attitude and 10 percent circumstance." The unspoken truth behind this pithy statement is that gaining the correct perspective is key to a positive attitude. Instead of forcing ourselves to have a positive attitude about broken moments by solely accepting the pain, look beyond the pain to the accompanying graciously provided beauty and light. A positive, grateful attitude will likely naturally follow.

As you read my story, you will often see the contrast between my hopeless feelings at different moments and my grateful perspective as I look back now. I encourage you to use recalibration questions to make your perspective on your own life one of gratitude and humility. My prayer is that this book will be one tool God uses to point you toward a deeper understanding of His unfailing grace in every moment—past, present, and future.

Part One

A DAY IN THE LIFE

Coping

Twenty-one minutes. The difference between a "normal" life and my life. I have agonized over these minutes many times.

Consistent interest from outside onlookers in how I overcome cerebral palsy to live a full life has always made me wonder if one day I would publish my story. However, the "when" was unclear. The first time I seriously considered myself emotionally and spiritually ready to write my life story without burden-minimizing platitudes was when I wrote this Facebook post on November 14, 2019:

> Yesterday I had to pay yet another unexpected disability-related expense. As I lay in bed, it didn't take long for my thoughts to spiral down: *This isn't fair. Why would God give me this good-for-nothing disability? Because of it, I have tens of thousands of dollars in medical expenses each year. I can't work full time. My neck and back hurt all the time. I can't play with my nieces and nephews the way I want. I can't make necessary calls to unfamiliar people on my own. I can't quickly grab my puppy and take her to the bathroom ...*

And the pity party went on for a few minutes of negative thoughts in rapid succession.

Then I thought, *Okay, Janae, you need to stop it. You know these thoughts don't help.* A prayer that Mom's family would sing before meals came to mind: "God is great, and God is good. And we thank Him for our food. By His hands, we all are fed. Give us Lord, our daily bread. Give us, Lord, our daily bread." I was convicted to be thankful to God for His provisions *today*. He doesn't need to give me provisions for tomorrow, because it's not here yet. Today I'm thankful that God provided enough to pay the expense; a job that keeps me off government assistance despite not working full time; bearable neck and back pain; nieces and nephews who love me; a highly competent mom and assistant to help me with calls; and a sweet puppy who is fairly easy to train. We won't always understand why, but a perspective of thankfulness is key to a joyful, peaceful life.

This almost instantaneous shift in perspective used to be beyond my grasp. My previous self would have indulged in self-pity and rapid questioning of God for far more than mere minutes. Instead of turning my gaze to His grace, I would have mulled over my depressive feelings for hours, days, and sometimes even months.

Although I quite love my life most days, it is not a life that an outside observer would naturally envy. My birth, though welcomed with all the familiar love that one could hope, resulted in irreversible postbirth complications. As I gasped for my first breath, my lungs didn't expand because they were surrounded by fluid. In the moments that followed, the doctors and nurses tried to discover the reason for my lack of breathing. At the time I was born, a newborn with fluid-engulfed lungs was a rare occurrence. The doctors checked for many other conditions prior to plunging a needle into my chest cavity as a last-ditch effort at saving this seemingly stillborn child.

Minutes. What if the doctors had drained the fluid a few minutes sooner? Would I be able to write with a pencil, albeit messily? Would I do my own hair and makeup, or brush my teeth without assistance? Would I speak clearly enough to carry on a casual conversation with a stranger?

Those first twenty-one minutes changed the whole trajectory of my life. Where was God and His grace during those moments? Was the golden thread present even at such a traumatic birth that resulted in seemingly dire consequences?

I was eventually diagnosed with athetoid cerebral palsy due to my postbirth complications. Athetoid cerebral palsy is difficult to treat and medicate. Other forms of cerebral palsy affect motor skills by making muscles either too tight or too loose. Therefore, treatments and medications are designed to either tighten or loosen muscles inverse to the respective cerebral palsy. However, athetoid cerebral palsy causes unpredictable muscle spasms. At any given moment, my muscles are either too tight or too loose to perform a task with the necessary coordination.

I would be lying if I said I don't question why God would allow me to have such a severe disability. Sometimes I also question, why, if He had to give me such a severe disability, did He spare my mind? Wouldn't it have been more merciful for Him to also give me a mental disability that would enable me to be less aware of my state of perpetual dependence on others?

Yet without fail, whenever I bring these questions to God, He gently reminds me of Job. You probably know the story. Job was a God-fearing man with an abundant life. God was so confident in Job's steadfast devotion that He allowed the devil to tempt Job via many hardships from loss of wealth and family to grave illness. At one point, Job questioned why God would allow such devastation in his life. God responded by asking Job a series of questions, all with answers pointing to the sovereignty of God.

"Where were you when I laid the earth's foundation?" (Job 38:4). "Who shut up the sea behind doors when it burst forth from the womb . . .?" (Job 38:8). "Have you ever given orders to the morning, or shown the dawn its place, that it might take the earth by the edges and shake the wicked out of it?" (Job 38:12–13). "Have you comprehended the vast expanses of the earth?" (Job 38:18). "Have you entered the storehouses of the snow . . .?" (Job 38:22).

In response to the answers to all these questions, I must yield and surrender to the sovereign will of God. I don't understand His all-powerful ways, so who am I to assume my ways are better? It isn't wrong to question God. In fact, I think He would rather have us question than simply live passively with no desire to understand. Yet when we do question God, and He reminds us of His sovereignty, at some point, faith must win. Faith in His goodness. Faith in His plan. Faith in His love. Faith.

When we arrive at a place where we're able to walk by faith, we trust God's plan for the hardships we don't understand. I'm steadfastly convinced that, in light of the natural consequences of this fallen world, God intends to use my cerebral palsy for His glory.

Volumes and volumes have been written on the problem of pain. I'm not a theologian qualified to give a dissertation on the subject. This is simply my story. Faith in His sovereignty despite my cerebral palsy has led me to recognize His grace even in the midst of suffering. I'm able to find small blessings throughout my days that would be nonexistent if not for my cerebral palsy.

For others to recognize the blessings of my cerebral palsy, I must be transparent about its complications. Expressing vulnerability about the complexities of my daily life didn't used to come naturally. My unwillingness to be vulnerable came from a great desire to appear as "normal" as possible. Interactions with my disabled peers only fueled this desire.

My parents quickly realized that although I struggled to fit in with my able-bodied peers, I also didn't easily fit in with other physically disabled children. This realization occurred after sending me to a summer camp for children with physical disabilities. I didn't enjoy the experience. The problem was that my parents hadn't raised me to be the type of preteen who would fit in with this group of peers. I'd been raised to be a confident and excited girl, capable of deep thoughts and conversations that expanded far beyond those of my disability. As a preteen concerned with fashion, boys, and pop music, I quickly found that my sense of humor was appreciated far more by the counselors than my fellow cabinmates, most of whose parents must have prioritized practicality over fashion when they selected their wardrobes. Needless to say, I only went to the camp for one year.

However, my emphasis on living "normally" often left me wanting to hide the parts of my life that are intrinsically "not normal." I felt overly embarrassed about the disability-related aspects of my life, including using adaptive technology in public. My junior high self was appalled at the thought of texting with my nose in public as I do now. Still, though I have come around to the cup and phone holders on my wheelchair, I still pride myself on refusing to wear baggy clothes or Velcro shoes merely for the sake of convenience.

When I was seven, Dad taught me how to dial the speakerphone with my nose so that I could call for help if necessary. I'd eventually use this technique to dial my friends all the time as well. I'm sure that my parents were torn between being proud of my independence and annoyed that I could now use the phone whenever I pleased. I definitely took full advantage of this freedom. When touch screens first came out, I knew that they'd become invaluable to my life. Moreover, when the software creators developed word prediction on these touch screen devices, my typing speed increased exponentially—the day of the software update was one of my few joyful days in law school. Thanks to Dad's creative thinking before touch screens were even common, I now text, reply to emails, and write, all with my nose. Some people must find the sight odd, but the only comments I receive are those expressing amazement. I had to humble myself enough to let go of my pride in being as normal as possible when I realized how essential being able to type in public, anywhere, anytime, was to my life.

Another aspect of my life that I used to be particularly self-conscious about was the fact that I need assistance in the bathroom. I only need minimal assistance since my mother incentivized me to learn how to pivot and transfer on my own with the promise that, once I could bear all my own weight, I could stop wearing the UFO braces on my feet. Until I was a sophomore in high school, I had to wear braces to assist with correct bone and tendon growth along with learning how to bear weight without my ankles twisting. However, the braces were shaped in a way that they only fit into large tennis shoes. So not only was it extremely uncomfortable to not be able to move my ankles all day, but these hideous items impeded my fashion for the first fifteen years of my life. Thankfully, Mom gave me a free pass on Sundays so I was able to wear cute shoes to church. Still, I blame my present obsession with shoes on years having only one pair of shoes to wear to school. God has abundantly blessed me with cute shoes in recent years even if I still can't wear high heels.

Yes, my love of shoes fueled my motivation to achieve transferring myself in the bathroom. However, I still need assistance with pulling up and down articles of clothing. Even if my hands were coordinated enough to maneuver my clothes, I need my hands to tightly grasp the grab bar to keep me from falling. The women who assist me frequently comment on my incredible bicep strength—they aren't wrong. Years of pulling myself in and out of bed and the shower, and on and off the toilet and couches, have resulted in biceps that are significantly stronger than the average woman. If they were any larger, they'd be obnoxious when buying tops.

Despite the blessing of biceps and being able to move my own body, from the time I was in junior high, I hated having others know that I needed assistance doing one of life's most private activities. When I attended school, I'd try my best to use the bathroom before the bell rang so that the halls of students wouldn't witness me coming out of the restroom with my para. If I wasn't able to convince her to wait until the second bell rang to open the door to the single-toilet bathroom, I had to emerge right into the middle of the crowd of students. The fact that there was only one toilet in the bathroom left no doubt in observers' minds that I did indeed require assistance with this intimate task.

When I went to college, my bathroom insecurity didn't dissipate as much as one might think. I was mortified at drawing attention to my need to have my friends assist me in using the bathroom and showering. *How will I ever get a one-on-one date if the guy is petrified that I might need to use the bathroom in the middle of the date?* You can't exactly go up to a guy at Bible college and say, "Hey, I know you haven't asked me out yet, but just in case you wanted to, no need to worry about how I'd use the bathroom on a date—I'll just dehydrate myself until we get back. It'll be great!"

When I online dated for a few years, I didn't have to worry about the guys being concerned with the bathroom situation because they only knew what I told them, and "Hey, I normally need assistance in the bathroom" is not exactly pre-date conversation material. By God's grace, I have developed innovative solutions to the problem of using the restroom on dates and when I'm home alone that don't involve perpetual dehydration—or, for those of you whose mind went there, adult diapers, which I don't intend to make a part of my wardrobe until I'm well in my upper nineties, thank you very much. I wonder how long God was waiting for me to figure out this simple solution: wear a dress.

I apologize if that was too much bathroom humor in one book, but people do seem overly concerned with my ability to manage my own bodily functions. I'll never forget my first attorney dinner at a large law firm. Even though I secured myself another attorney as a date, the event coordinator was so concerned about me going to the event without my assistant that I had to endure the most awkward conversation of my life with someone who knew almost nothing about me:

"Janae, I heard you have a date for the dinner."
"Yep, I'm excited!"
"You know you can bring an assistant to help you."
"I'll be fine."
"How will you get there?"
"He'll drive me."
"He can't help you in the bathroom, can he?"

Resisting the urge to say, "No, duh, I'm not going to have my date help me in the bathroom. You know, I have had cerebral palsy for a while now, I think I factored in the bathroom situation when deciding to bring a date instead of my assistant. Would you really like me to go into the dirty details of how I plan to handle my bodily functions?" I simply smiled and replied, "I'll be fine."

I endured a confused stare for a few long moments until the conversation ended. Sometimes well-meaning people say the most offensive things of all. But as much as these comments infuriate me by implying that I'm not intelligent enough to handle my own bathroom needs, I must choose to give grace as God has given me grace.

Mom is the one who most frequently reminds me to give these ignorant people grace. As much as I may not want to hear her advice in the moment when I'm venting, she's right. It is far better to look at people with grace than to let your anger boil over at them. What good would lashing out at them do? Some people are just not going to understand our lives. But giving grace doesn't mean that we can't recognize the humor in the situation with those closest to us. In this case, it's inherently humorous for someone to assume that a professional and educated woman who has been dealing with limitations her whole life wouldn't have a plan for handling her bathroom needs at a professional event.

The younger Janae would be mortified that I told you that embarrassing story. I wouldn't have been so comfortable sharing the complexities of living with cerebral palsy. But, for you, my beloved readers, I'll be vulnerable for the sake of showing the magnitude of God's goodness in light of my devastatingly severe debilitations.

Living

Hands—I absolutely hate the look of my hands. They're genetically large hands, but they're also extremely beat up from using them for daily activities while not having the coordination necessary to be gentle enough not to scrape them up. If my fingernails get too long, my clenching hand spasms will cause my nails to cut my skin. When I type on a computer instead of a touch screen, I must single-poke keys through a keyguard on an adaptive keyboard with my knuckles. Having my left hand in a fist allows me more efficient control over what I type than when I type with my fingertips. As a result, the knuckles on my left hand are swollen and covered with callouses. Not as attractive as one might like.

Hands—I need my big, tough hands from the moment I awake. God knew. As much as I hate their appearance, to the extent that I avoid nail polish to keep from drawing attention to them, I love my hands. My bed has a metal headboard with bars that I can easily grasp. When I awake, I grasp my headboard, pivot my legs over to the edge of the bed, and pull myself up before standing to pivot to my wheelchair that's parked parallel to my bed. Even with all of my bouts of depression, I've never failed to get out of bed. I consider this a great feat. Sometimes it takes a few hours longer. Sometimes I had to tell myself, "Don't think about what is next. Just get out of bed." Other times I prayed in desperation, "God, please just give me the strength to get out of bed." By God's grace, I've never spent an entire day in bed due to one of my depression episodes.

Maybe I should mention that there's typically another person in the room when I awake. Hello! Nothing like having company first thing in the morning. Once I literally drag myself out of bed, my caregiver assists me in dressing, which I can't accomplish on my own even if efficiency weren't a factor. We then move to the bathroom sink, where she brushes my teeth, styles my hair, and applies my makeup before placing the jewelry on me that I select. Until finding my permanent assistant, the mornings were a gamble. If my caregiver was talented with hair and makeup, I gazed in the mirror with relieved pleasure and confidence for the day. If she wasn't as talented, I found solace in the lack of public appearances of the day or the fact that my next caregiver might be skilled enough to fix it.

Once I'm physically ready for the day, we proceed to the kitchen where she prepares and feeds me breakfast. I often wonder what it would feel like to walk out to my kitchen alone, cook an egg, toast bread, and sit down to enjoy a quiet devotional at my dining room table over breakfast. As it is, I either have to invite her to join in on my devotions to avoid awkward silence or have my devotions after her departure.

Since founding my own law firm and hiring Sharalee, who I consider a relatively permanent assistant, my mornings have gotten better. Not only do I wake up later, but also, I never dread having to make morning conversation. Seeing her cheerful face and hearing her chipper voice almost instantaneously sets a bright tone for the day—albeit she has already been up taking care of her family for hours before I even open my eyes.

Until I founded my own law firm, early mornings were a part of life. Most caregivers didn't try to make conversation first thing in the morning because, like me, they weren't typically morning people either. Still, every few years, I had a caregiver who either felt the need to make conversation or simply enjoyed morning chatter. One time I had a caregiver who continually asked me, "What has God been teaching you lately?" Mind you, many times this question surfaced before we even made our way to the breakfast table. Sometimes she asked this well-intended question while the toothbrush was still in my mouth. This gave my tired, crabby, morning brain enough time to come up with the secretly humorous response of "Patience." Of course, only God and I knew what I meant.

Not all peppy morning caregivers annoy me forever. One of my *now* best friends, Stephanie, began working for me during my senior year of college—August 2012. On her first morning shift, she flung open the door to my dorm room, excitedly exclaiming in her loud, joyful voice, "It's a great day to be alive!" Note that this was during training week for student leaders, meaning that we were up at 7:00 a.m. and awake until 2:00 a.m. preparing for the upcoming school year. (I'm sure we also spent a fair amount of time goofing off in the way that college students tend to do.) Regardless, I wasn't only tired but also concerned about having this wake-up call for the next nine months. After she said, "It's a great day to be alive!" I promptly flung the blanket over my head and said, "Or dead." Either I was more comfortable with her than most from the beginning, or I lacked some of the tactfulness I have now.

≈

Given that I'm a type A perfectionist, I'm eager to complete household chores. During the hours I have caregivers, I complete all of the tasks of a normal woman running her household. I'm the brain. My caregivers are the hands. We do laundry, clean, and grocery shop. I can't drive myself, so I must make sure that I complete all my errands when I have someone to chauffeur me.

I have chosen to find joy in my inability to do chores or drive by adopting Anne of Green Gables' imagination (a favorite of my childhood books). Whenever I'm frustrated that I can't just clean my own house, throw in the laundry at midnight, or drive wherever the wind takes me, I imagine that I'm a princess or wealthy duchess. Princesses and ladies of wealth don't do their own chores or drive themselves. So I find thankfulness that I can hire help to do these tasks, although I'm not a woman of great wealth. How fun to have someone style your hair and makeup every day! How nice that I don't have to clean my own house or do my laundry. If I choose, I see grace even in these moments when I'm tempted to chaff at all the tasks I want to do on my own, but can't.

Beyond chores and work, I enjoy time with friends and family just as much as the average person. One of my favorite days is Friday. As you will read, my disability prevents me from working five days a week. I don't work Fridays. Fridays are Mom days. Mom and I spend the day running errands, shopping for fun, and, our favorite thing, eating lunch out. Mom was wise enough to come up with "Fun Fridays" when I first cut back at work. Depression overwhelmed me when I cut back my hours in my position at a large law firm. I felt like a failure. I wasn't measuring up in my mind. Mom, eager to help however she could, knew that spending Fridays together gave me something else to focus on for those hours—like a bear coming out of a dark cave into the sunlight reflected off of a clear stream, Fridays were always a patch of sun.

My friends also make an effort to visit me. I say "make an effort" because spending time with me requires effort. Except for the rare occasions when I have a caregiver to drop me off and stick around long enough to drive me home, my friends must drive to me. There's rarely a "grab a quick lunch," "see you at the movies," or "meet me at the mall." Instead, it's "I'll bring you lunch," "I'll pick you up for the movie," or "I'll swing by to get you on the way to the mall." This is more difficult for me to deal with than simply being unable to drive for my own errands. I feel bad about being an inconvenience to my friends. If I'm not careful, my thoughts can spiral downward into discouragement over the fact that my friends must make more efforts on my behalf.

Their efforts aren't limited to driving me. They also must feed me, assist me in the restroom, and deal with people who stare and make unintelligible comments. These people are a part of my everyday life, so they're also a part of the lives of my friends and family. My friends frequently express anger when people stare at me until years of friendship build up their tolerance to this behavior. As my best friend, Heather, said, "I used to literally want to punch everyone who reacted poorly to you when we were in public."

As just one example of the scenarios to which Heather was referring, my friend, Becca, and I went to a hotel to write the majority of this book. One morning when we were eating breakfast in the lobby area, a young server came up to the table where Becca was feeding me.

"Mmm, that's good, huh?" the server said.

I looked at her with a smile, as a smile is usually enough to make these people go on their way. I kept eating.

"She really likes that French toast, doesn't she?"

Becca, angry at this inferior treatment of me, simply said, "Yep."

We ignored her until she stopped staring and walked away. Afterward, Becca confided in me that she wanted to say, "Yes, and she's also an attorney who is here writing her first book!"

All my friends have felt this way at one time or another. Yet they keep taking me out, knowing that there will always be more people who assume I'm mentally slow. They must come to peace with these prejudices against me in order to enjoy our friendship. Like me, they must reconcile their desire to defend my intelligence with the need to show others grace.

While days with my friends and family bring much joy, I also find joy in the solitude of my home. You might be surprised to know that I own my own home. When I first decided it was time to buy a house, I did so with fear. I anticipated that I'd purchase my first home with my husband. Yet as I neared twenty-eight with no marital prospects, financial prudence dictated that buying a house was likely the next responsible step. I was fearful not only because I was single, but also because I believed finding an accessible house within my budget would be a long, difficult journey. Yet in the end, my disability actually helped me by limiting my options to the extent that little doubt existed when I found the one. God showed up in an unbelievably clear way.

I first began toying with the idea of buying at the end of November. I remember because the first day that I thought seriously about the idea was the day Dad had knee-replacement surgery. My poor parents begged me to wait a while. I intended to take their advice. I really did. Mom cautioned me that finding the right house would take anywhere from six months to a year.

Perfect, I thought, *I'll start looking in January, buy a house between June and October, and Dad's knee will be all better by the time I move.* Being me, who is meticulous with her finances and budgeting, I obviously needed to see the type of loan I could get before I started looking at houses. Within the first week of January, I was approved for a sizable loan. I enlisted the help of a real estate agent. Mom agreed to look at houses with me on Friday of the following week.

Mom insisted that I could find a small house that would work with my wheelchair. Mom is rarely wrong, but I knew she was just flat-out wrong on this one. However, being an attorney, I knew the proof would be in the pudding. Unbeknownst to her, I agreed to see the only seven houses within my area and budget that had one bedroom and one bathroom on the main level. Most of the houses were small. I knew I didn't want them, but I needed to prove a point. With no prior coaching from me, my agent took us to the smallest houses first. This must have been divine grace, because Mom was quickly able to see the extensive and expensive remodeling required to even make these houses livable. Even with remodeling, the houses would never be ideal. For example, small houses have small bathrooms that can't accommodate wheelchairs in any comfortable way.

As we toured the small houses, I could see that Mom was coming to understand my point of view. When we drove up to a spacious townhome, I could hear the hallelujah chorus. Before we had even gotten out of the car, I told Mom, "I have a good feeling about this one."

She laughed at me because this was the first big house we were going to see. "Of course, you do," she said with a chuckle.

When we realized that this was the first house that I could already drive my power wheelchair into, the chorus got louder, and I got more excited. One of the downsides of my disability is that hiding my emotions is difficult because my facial muscles don't cooperate with my desire to remain poised. Thankfully, my facial muscles have become more cooperative on most occasions after years of training. Apparently, my excitement at this house couldn't be contained. My agent found my jittering body, wide-eyed smile, flushed face, and high-pitched voice quite humorous. Wouldn't you be excited about finding a house that wouldn't require building a ramp just to get into the front door?

My first view of the interior confirmed it—I wanted this house. When we opened the front door, I realized that the hallelujah chorus was coming from inside. My eyes took in the wood floors, high ceilings, and the beautiful fireplace.

Immediately, the silent praying began—okay, it was more begging at first. It took me a few hours to pray "Thy will," but I eventually came around. At the end of the tour, it became clear that the only remodeling required was to make the entrances to the master bedroom, bathroom, and closet wider—pretty small potatoes compared to the remodels necessary on the other houses.

We had to act fast. I say "we" because I certainly wasn't

going to buy a house without the blessing of my parents. Maybe I would have felt differently if I wasn't disabled. However, as things sat, I knew they would have to assist with not only moving and remodeling but also upkeep. I tried to minimize this burden for them by purchasing a townhome with snow removal and lawn care included in the HOA fees. Still, any way you sliced it, I would need their help on this new endeavor.

By the next day, after many discussions with my parents, I put in an offer. An open house that day brought in another offer. After a twenty-hour bidding war, with much praying and soul searching on whether I really trusted God no matter the outcome, the homeowner accepted my bid. I was almost a homeowner merely a week after I'd officially started the hunt and after just one day of looking at houses. I felt bad for Dad with his knee, but we all agreed that this house was too good to pass up. Dad was able to enlist the help of my younger brother and cousin with the remodel.

Owning a house has been wonderful, but it has also made me aware of new limitations as well. Unless I become wealthy enough to hire a landscaper, my yard will never be anything special. Sadly, my expectations of the lawn care included in my homeowner's association dues were far too high. Dues cover mowing and fertilizing, which is so nice but far from the lawn care provided by my apartment complex. My naive perspective caught me off guard, because when I bought my townhome, I didn't expect to worry about the exterior of my home at all.

This year, Mom wanted to plant flowers, lay mulch, and trim bushes around my house. However, between managing my caregivers, working as an attorney, and only having so many hours of help with living activities, I simply don't have the capacity to manage yardwork, especially if I desire energy for a social life. My lack of a green thumb is nothing new since buying a house—I cringe whenever someone gives me a plant. I understand the intention behind the gift. In fact, my own mother refuses to stop buying me plants, insisting that they are life-giving. From my perspective, plants are just inanimate objects that I don't love that I must take responsibility for. If I fail, they die. Being the perfectionist that I am, I have enough to worry about without adding plants to my list. This is not to say I don't love flowers. Buy me all the precut flowers in the world, and I'll gladly accept the challenge of keeping them lively for a week, knowing that when they do wilt, it's not my fault. Better yet, buy me beautiful fake flowers and plants.

Another limitation became apparent when I couldn't decorate my whole house in a weekend:

> When you are a go-getter, type A person who physically can't decorate or organize yourself, moving into a new house means an unexpected lesson in patience. But it also means celebrating the little milestones that your friends and family help you accomplish. As of tonight, my bedroom is complete thanks to my wonderful mom and sister-in-law! I feel like this house is a great analogy for many things in life— we can either focus on the positive aspects or fret about the nuances that we can literally do nothing about at the moment (in my case, an unorganized closet, unpainted bathroom, messy guest room full of boxes, and decor that has yet to be hung). I understand that these are minor annoyances in the grand scheme of things but I'm surprised at this somewhat new CP-imposed inconvenience catching me off guard. Like, "What? I can't just go to Lowe's by myself and paint my bathroom until 2:00 a.m.?" Still, like every other minor CP-imposed inconvenience in my otherwise

amazing life, I must choose to focus on joy instead of fixating on the unfixable.

—March 1, 2019

All in all, owning my own home has been a joy. Even with the learning curve, I find myself appreciating how homeownership stretches and develops my trust and faith in God. Anxiety about the yard and other household projects could overwhelm me. However, whether trusting Him to provide people to care for my physical needs or help out around the house, I must choose to walk forward in faith instead of being paralyzed by fear. The next moment of His grace is soon to follow.

≈

The fact that I have such a nice place to live is one reason I enjoy evenings at home.

My caregivers come to assist me with eating dinner, showering, and getting ready for bed. I usually eat takeout for dinner. I have gotten over my deep-rooted perception that I should cook for many reasons.

First, I can't actually cook. If anyone has an excuse to depart from homemade-dinner-every-night roots, it's the woman who isn't coordinated enough to mix ingredients, use knives, or handle hot pans. Mom did a great job teaching me the basics, but cooking is a difficult art to refine without actually doing. For a while, I tried to direct caregivers in the kitchen, but the whole ordeal wore me out. And so, I hung up my apron after proving I could direct the baking of a superior white-chocolate-raspberry cheesecake and cooking of homemade meals, such as grilled chicken with a side of potatoes, bread, and vegetables. I guess my pride wanted to prove my womanhood in the traditional sense. I'm glad that God continues to cultivate my humility in a way that gives freedom to be who I am and live the way that makes sense for me.

Second, I'm single, meaning that cooking even a fourth of a recipe would likely mean multiple meals of the same food. Freezing is an option, but even freezers are only so big. I like more variety than rotating between the same five dishes in the freezer for twenty meals.

Third, I have to pay a caregiver by the hour to cook for me. It makes more financial sense to have 1.5 fewer hours of help per night and order takeout prepared by a professional chef than to pay unexperienced college-student cooks to attempt to prepare something edible. Okay, that was a little dramatic—but I'm sure that none of my caregivers object to the fact that I don't expect them to cook food that is sophisticated, tasteful, and healthy. I do, however, trust them to make sandwiches and pasta.

Finally, being an attorney is hard. Being a single female attorney with a disability is even harder. Thus, the fact that I can afford to eat takeout 90 percent of the time by dividing the meals into thirds and supplementing them with fresh fruits is one small motivation to stay employed. It's the simple joys in life—like knowing you will have a perfectly grilled half of a burger for dinner.

〜

By the end of the day, I'm usually quite fatigued. I count this as a blessing because I don't desire to go out even if I could drive. Most of the time, while my friends are enjoying evenings with their significant others and children, I'm quite content to enjoy a quiet evening at home in the company of my beloved pets.

God provided me with two furry companions who love me. Miss Molly is my three-year-old cat who I adopted from my parents' acreage when she was a kitten. She's tidy and easy to care for. My mom advised me against adding a cat to my life. It is hard enough to take care of myself, let alone an animal. Strangely enough, I find that caring for a cat is easier than keeping plants alive. I adopted Miss Molly when I was going through my worst depression. She immensely helped my mood and loneliness. For a cat, she's extremely affectionate, greeting me by the door, frequently finding her way to whatever room I'm in, and curling up by my face at night. One evening, I was crying into my pillow. Although I'm sure she didn't fully understand her actions, she put her paw on my cheek and dried a tear away. She also becomes greatly distressed when I'm in trouble. For example, if I fall, she paces the room until I get back up.

But Miss Molly is still a cat. After I bought my house, I found myself longing for a dog like the one I'd had growing up. My parents brought home Honey when I was three. At first, Mom objected to the idea of adding a dog to her already chaotic life of raising small children. However, it didn't take much convincing for her to selflessly adopt this free mutt. Plus, Honey only ever lived outside, making things slightly easier.

As I grew, so did my love for Honey. Initially, I crawled around with her on the deck, playing with and petting her for hours. Until this point, I'd been terrified of dogs because they jumped up on me. Unlike other kids, I was sitting low to the ground with no ability to run away. Honey knew how to be gentle with me. I don't ever remember her knocking me over as we played. When I outgrew playing on the ground, she followed me on all my electric-wheelchair walks around our acreage. She frequently placed her head in my lap so I could pet her. Many of my sad schooldays ended with me finding comfort in stroking her soft fur. I intended to take a senior picture with her, but she passed at the age of fourteen, just a few months before the pictures.

From then on, I knew I wanted a dog when I grew up. As with Miss Molly, Mom advised against getting a puppy. I again didn't abort my mission to find the perfect canine companion. I did, however, heed Mom's advice on the type of dog—a Cavapoo, which is a medium-sized hypoallergenic breed that doesn't shed. True to my mother's nature, when I make a decision, she supports me even if she doesn't agree—as long as it doesn't contradict God's word. True to my nature, when I decide on a course of action, I make it happen in short order. No sooner had I warmed Mom up to the idea than had I put a deposit down on a female Cavapoo born just a few days prior.

Eight weeks and a chunk of change later, I brought home my bundle of joy, Rosie—my first very own dog. I was thrilled and nervous. As in every other area of my life, major adaptations to dog ownership were required due to my cerebral palsy. First, I knew that letting her out to use the bathroom in the backyard would be too unpredictable, even with an electric fence. When a dog, especially a puppy, is outside, too many uncertainties exist for someone with very impaired motor skills to be unaccompanied by another. Thus, per the suggestion of my wise mother, Rosie's bathroom is located in my garage on a rotating potty pad. By God's grace, my house has more than one door leading in from the garage. Installing a doggie door and fencing off the small area outside that door in the garage was easy and not a traffic inconvenience. I don't have to worry about having someone with me every three or four hours to let her out.

The next challenge was her feeding schedule. My caregiver schedule doesn't always line up with when Rosie needs to eat. Again, I thank God for technology because I found an automatic timed feeder and water dispenser. Problem easily solved. It took me longer to solve the problem of how to walk Rosie frequently enough. Cavapoos are supposed to be calm—the jury is still out on this one because she's still a puppy. She needs exercise. A tired puppy is a good puppy. Unfortunately, I soon realized that her stamina to play fetch long outlasts my arm's stamina. I didn't want to buy a dog treadmill—I wasn't raised to be the type of person who buys a dog treadmill. However, when you are disabled in a way that keeps you from taking your puppy for a walk on your own, and you can't just let her run in your backyard, you quickly become the person who buys a dog treadmill. Mom rolled her eyes and laughed, but admitted its practicality.

Since getting Rosie, more than ever, I have bemoaned my unquenchable tenacity and unwillingness to allow my cerebral palsy to keep me from living the life I desire. Why do I love dogs? Why couldn't I just settle for owning a cat and a house? "You just had to complicate your life with a puppy, didn't you, Janae?" I shake my head at myself. "Mom was right this time."

Yet I find myself overcome with unbelievable love and gratefulness for this puppy who is naughty half of the time. Though I may never have children, I feel that I understand the struggles of early parenthood so much better since Rosie came into my life: the tension between discipline and grace; the begging to play when I'm tired or busy; the constant need for attention; and the messes in my previously immaculately clean house. Further, I understand how God must feel when I refuse to obey Him. Like me, He must sigh, "Why don't you understand that I'm not doing this to punish you? I'm doing this for your own good. Stop running away from me."

Don't get the wrong idea. Rosie's sweet. She's the sweetest when it's just me, her, and Miss Molly. While she makes my caregivers chase her, she's usually quite responsive to what I want her to do when we're alone. She knows I can't chase her. She is also calmer when we're alone—curling up next to my wheelchair as I work at my computer, or burrowing herself in the covers next to me as I lay in bed.

It is during these moments when I'm grateful for my unquenchable tenacity, which brings complications but also blissful moments that I wouldn't miss for the world. My God-given driven spirit allows me to fully and joyfully live a day in my life despite all of the obstacles, whether physical or emotional. As a result, I'm able to see abundant moments of grace in most of life's days, reflected beautifully through the cracks pointing toward eternity.

~~~

On a few occasions, I have spent a day alone. I know what you are thinking: *A day alone? How is that possible? That seems to go against everything she has written so far about her disability.* Mom wishes you were right. When she raised such an independent daughter, I'm not sure she thought about the consequences on her nerves. Good thing she's a woman of faith.

Yes. When I was twenty-five years old, my stubborn independence reached a new high, and I decided that I wanted to spend the whole day—over thirty-six hours—alone. This was quite surprising considering that I used to be afraid to even sleep in my apartment without my roommate. As God would orchestrate, my first roommate was home most of the time, but my second roommate was gone a great deal. With my first roommate, whenever she was gone from the apartment for a night, I likely either had someone over to stay with me or went to my parents' for the night. Thankfully, my second roommate was gone so often that I figured out that I was perfectly capable of spending the night alone. Further, if my second roommate hadn't been gone as much, I would have never realized that I do in fact have the ability to live alone as long as caregivers come at regular intervals.

When I was twenty-four, I moved into my first apartment alone. This meant that whenever I couldn't find a caregiver, Mom had to check on me to make sure I was alive. One time I didn't have a caregiver on a Sunday, but I knew Mom was extremely busy. I elected to go it alone. Before my Saturday caregiver left, I instructed her to put out double doses of my pills, change me into a dress that I could also sleep in, prepare and refrigerate bags of bite-size food that didn't need to be heated, and, of course, put my caffeinated drinks for the next day open on the table.

This was before I became a dog-and-cat mom. Now, I also ensure that my pets had food and water set out for the next day. But back then, things were simpler. After I had her set out everything, I was good to go. Thanks to my dress, I had no problem using the bathroom on my own. I slept in my glasses so I wouldn't have to worry about putting them back on. The next morning, after eating my prepeeled oranges and caffeinated drink, I watched church online before devouring my lunch of deli meat and crackers. When I made it through the entire day, I felt quite accomplished even though my hair was a complete mess and I wasn't presentable in any fashion.

Although I've promised Mom that I'll only spend a day alone as a last, last resort, the empowerment that I gained from that day is invaluable. I praise God for the ability to take care of myself when I need to. I'm no longer fearful of caregivers canceling at the last minute, because I know I'll be at least okay. I can hydrate myself by filling an insulated mug with faucet water run through the small hole in the top. I rest assured that my pets will be fed and watered thanks to the modern technology of automated feeders. My phone, which syncs with my iPad and computer, ensures that I can call for help if I need it. The new fad in food delivery allows me to order food right to my door. Sushi has proven to be the easiest delivered meal to feed myself. Don't worry—I have mastered the art of sleeping with my long hair in a tight bun and long dresses so that I won't scare the poor delivery driver.

Finally, and most recently, I discovered a new approach to eyeglasses that has significantly increased my independence. Although I would love to undergo eye surgery to eliminate the need for glasses, I'm not currently a viable candidate given the measurements of my cornea combined with my astigmatism. Beyond the other drawbacks of leave-in contacts, my muscle spasms make having someone help me put the contacts in my eye significantly more dangerous. That leaves good old-fashioned glasses. Until my most recent pair, I got wraparound earpieces to keep the glasses from falling off. However, now that I'm older and primarily sitting in a chair all day, I discovered that the normal earpieces are usually enough to keep the glasses on. This was a critical discovery because now I can put my glasses on myself by placing them lens down, temples open on my bed, and face-planting into them. My initial face plant avoids scratching the lens due to the soft bedding supporting the glasses, but gets the glasses on to my face in a secure enough way for me to sit up and push them on to my nose bridge the rest of the way. These faceplants may shorten the lifespan of my glasses, but thank God for creative thinking.

Working

I'm an attorney. You already know this. Reading that I was a totally disabled individual who practices law might be the whole reason you picked up this book. Most people find my profession utterly perplexing in light of my cerebral palsy. Some are impressed.

Yet I can tell that others don't quite believe that I'm actually an attorney:

> People who know me really well or who have read my written work sometimes forget that the majority of the world has a deep-rooted belief that I'm not intelligent due to my speech impediment. Today I was reminded of this prejudice when my neighbor, who I previously told I was an attorney, came over to ask a quick question and asked my assistant in a hushed voice right in front of me: "Can she understand me?" But, even when my assistant reiterated that I was intelligent, my neighbor talked to me in a loud voice.
>
> I share this not to make her look bad, but to encourage you to be aware that the people you assume are unintelligent may be the opposite. For me, I don't get upset about this faulty assumption anymore. Still, it's a constant discouragement when trying to develop a plan for networking to bring new clients to my firm. Networking is hard enough for the average attorney without having to overcome the assumption that you aren't even as intelligent as the average second-grader. I must continue to trust God to pave the way and find my identity in Him.
>
> —August 30, 2019

The previous descriptions of outings with my friends have already clued you in on the fact that people underestimating my intelligence is a common occurrence. I wish I could tell you that I'm always gracious with ignorant people, but I'm not. Sometimes I get angry:

> So I go to a credit card table with Katie Loewen and the woman proceeds to talk to Katie, asking her if I

know what a credit card is. I sit there thinking, *Oh my word, I took the stinking LSATS, I think I know what a credit card is.* I mildly recovered from this annoyance when I heard my favorite joke ever about me (sarcasm). Someone made the oh-so-not-funny-since-I-was-seven speed-limit joke. To which I thought, *If you want to drive a sensitive machine that takes three seconds to come to a stop, with an arm that has a spasm every five seconds, be my guest.*

However, the light of this situation is that God showed me I still have much to learn about patience, compassion, and a nonjudgmental attitude. I hope you have a good laugh from this status—I did.

—October 9, 2012

Even at extended family get-togethers, I get angry when no one cares to listen to my perspective on either law or theology. Sometimes, even if they do listen, I feel as if they are still unsure whether I know what I'm talking about—despite knowing full well that I graduated top of my class from law school and work as a licensed attorney. Whether this feeling is accurate or not, if I'm not focused on Christ, the feeling produces anger.

When I'm focused on Christ, 2 Corinthians 12:7 comes to mind: "Therefore, in order to keep me from becoming conceited, I was given a thorn in my flesh . . ." My disability definitely keeps me humble in all areas of life. When I slip into pride about how good of a person I am, I remember all that I can't do for others. I can't help my mom cook Thanksgiving dinner. I can't spontaneously clean my friend's house when she's having a bad week. Instead of taking pride in my acts of service for others, I must humbly let them help me. It's quite difficult to stay conceited when you must be fed, dressed, and bathed by someone else.

This somewhat forced humility also extends to my career in

that I simply can't do most jobs. I wanted to be a teacher. This is the occupation I first remember desiring apart from motherhood. I then wanted to be a nurse. Mom was a nurse. Even in my preteens, I realized that both these occupations were impossible due to my cerebral palsy. I couldn't speak clearly enough to instruct a classroom. My hands were too unsteady to insert an IV.

I wanted to be an architect. I could create many designs with the eight mouse arrows of my keyboard. Then I realized, while the mouse arrows allowed me to run the computer as needed by the average operator, I would never be able to make the necessary swoops in designs with my mouse arrows. As you might suspect by now, I don't have the ability to operate a regular mouse or trackpad. My irregular movements and muscle spasms make positioning the cursor on any intended point too difficult. Still, I'm fortunate enough that mouse keys with adjustable speeds were invented. Mouse keys are essential to my use of a computer. However, unfortunately, when I desired to be a graphic designer, I quickly ran into the same problem as when I desired to be an architect—the mouse keys don't make creating designs with curved lines possible. Sure, I could insert curved lines and adjust their angles and measurements. But, even at a young age, I knew that this adaptation would put me at an insurmountable disadvantage to my peer architects and graphic designers.

I shifted my focus to written professions—accountants and journalists. However, again I realized that my typing speed of seven words a minute along with my speech impediment put me at a disadvantage to my peers that I was unsure I could overcome. After all, entry-level accountants and journalists are rarely given assistants to help with typing and verbal communications. As you will see in the section on Dad, at this point is when he first encouraged me to become a lawyer. From that point on, God seemed to pave the way even in the midst of all my doubts:

Janae Hofer

Janae Hofer is going into law?

—October 25, 2008

The Future—Dun dun dun
I'm not a big fan of change. That doesn't seem to keep from happening. In nine months, everything will be different. I'm going to Grace University next year. Yes, I'm moving out. On top of that, I'm going to do a prelaw co-op program with UNO. Don't worry——I'm going to be a research lawyer. Minimal talking skills required. Being the overly organized person that I am, I already know that if I attend law school, it will be at Creighton. The sad part about all of these plans is that they can change. I like to know where my life is headed, uncertainty annoys me. This is when I have to stop and remember God is in control. My end destination is heaven. What I do along the way is merely a road leading me there.

—December 2, 2008

On Saturday, for the first time since beginning law school, I found myself genuinely looking forward to the future without trying to force myself to be hopeful. I'm so excited to see what God has in store for me after the next eighteen months. After I become a licensed attorney, I may or may not practice law. The truth is I work hard, but I don't love law, and I'm bad at law school because it isn't set up for someone who can't physically write, and I can't remember every word that professors say. So I may do the whole corporate America thing, or I may do the broke writer thing. I don't know what I want to be when I grow up, but can't wait to see where God leads.

—October 14, 2014

After accepting a job offer ten months ago, I'm happy to say that I'll finally be starting as an attorney at [the firm] in one week. Today I was notified that I passed the Nebraska Bar Exam, which was my final hurdle to becoming an attorney. As all you who have been following my posts over the years know, becoming an attorney has been a long, difficult road. I'm thankful that God got me through it, and I attribute all glory to Him because I wanted to quit many times. I thank my parents for pushing me and supporting me, my grandparents and family for praying, and my friends for listening to me vent and cry. I'll be sworn in on April 21, so look for pictures.

—April 8, 2016

Yes, God led me, at times kicking and screaming, to the career I have now. I think God knew the platform of my career coupled with my traumatic disability for my words of His grace to have the most impact.

Practicing as an attorney with the right assistant, the disadvantages associated with my disability are substantially mitigated. As I projected, once I distinguished myself with my law school class ranking, the law firm that hired me was willing to pay for my assistant. However, this was only possible because my parents generously footed the bill for my assistant during my clerkship at a Fortune 500 company while I was in law school. God seemed to bless our calculated steps in that I only applied for one clerkship in law school.

This narrow application decision wasn't out of pride on my part, but out of insecurity. My law school hosted an open house for firms and corporations seeking to hire law clerks the January after I began law school. Sitting squarely in the top ten percent of my class, my faithful assistant Kersten and I set out to the open house armed with my polished resume. We went from table to table, attempting to speak with the representatives and hand out my resume for consideration. Following the open house, law students were supposed to apply for various clerkships. Each time I approached a representative, I saw the uncertainty in their eyes. I could read the message behind their polite smiles as I offered my unsteady hand to shake and introduced myself in my slurred voice that Kersten had to interpret. The faces all read the same: *What is she doing here? We will never hire her, but better be polite so we won't get sued.* After I handed each representative my resume, their faces changed to surprise, only confirming my earlier readings of their expressions. Even then, they seemed eager to end interactions with me.

"Should we go?" I asked Kersten as we sat on a law school bench after receiving the same reaction from every representative thus far.

"It's up to you," she said in her ever-supportive voice. I hadn't even wanted to come to this silly open house. I'd known I would be treated like this. Yet I felt like God wanted me to go, so begrudgingly I went.

Okay, God, I'm here—I'm not only still in law school, but I'm here at this open house that I didn't want to go to for the very reason that, even with my stellar grades, I can't compete with these other charismatic law students. What do you want me to do now? I looked over to see the Union Pacific booth. *Hey, my uncle is pretty high up in Union Pacific. I always saw myself working for a company big enough to accommodate my disability*, I thought.

"Let's talk to Union Pacific and then leave," I told Kersten. As God would have it, the Union Pacific representative was the only one who was warm and welcoming to me. After speaking with her about the clerkship, I went home to draft my cover letter and apply. Of course, wisdom dictated that I enlist the help of my uncle to put in a good word for me prior to the first interview. Lest anyone think I obtained the clerkship strictly upon the good word of my uncle, a few years later my uncle again put in a good word for me in reference to a permanent position. I didn't even get called for an interview.

When I received the call for my clerkship interview, I was shocked and overjoyed. I, and my sharpest assistant, Ella, put on our Sunday best and aced the interview. Ella had volunteered to be my assistant at the beginning of my clerkship, which was instrumental to my success. She was my first work assistant, setting the gold standard for all future work assistants. Her intelligence made dictation seamless. Her pleasant and captivating demeanor reflected well on us as a team. She proved to be so invaluable to me that when I applied for my first post-law-school attorney position, I paid her a hefty amount of money to accompany me to both interviews even though she was no longer working for me at the time.

> Dear friends and family,
> I'm excited to announce that I accepted a job offer to be an *attorney* at [a respected Omaha law firm]. I'll begin after I graduate and pass the bar exam, which will be around April. Words can't express how I feel. I'm humbled and amazed. For seven years, I trusted God in blind faith, knowing that if it didn't work out, I would look like the biggest fool ever. I had to deal with the doubts of others along with my own doubts. But God always had a plan. I'm excited to see where my new journey will take me. I want to thank my parents (Curt Hofer and Linda Hofer) for their love and support that got me to this point. I also want to thank Ella Stewart for missing work to assist me in

both interviews. Finally, thank you to all of you who have encouraged and supported me through the years.

—July 14, 2015

That is just how God has worked. He doesn't always provide me with the best assistants, but He provides me with who I need in the interims between the bests. I got the clerkship at Union Pacific. The clerkship provided me with the connections I needed to obtain a position as an associate attorney at a large firm that I held for four years prior to opening my own law firm.

∼

When I began writing this book, I had a completely different perspective on my career as an attorney. This is because I was still working as a corporate litigation attorney at a large firm. Simply put, my career not only made me feel dead inside, but I found no genuine pride in my profession. Superficial pride gave me a slight buzz, but I knew that defending corporations against cancer victims and their widows was a far cry from what I envisioned for my life. Regardless of whether the corporations were actually liable for the cancer, I felt like the attorney villain in every movie and TV show, the butt of every lawyer joke ever told.

Needless to say, I didn't have many opportunities to work with ministries or nonprofits. When I originally decided to pursue law, I made the decision from a practical and financially responsible standpoint. However, I would be disingenuous if I didn't also recognize that my desire to minister to people has outweighed my desire to practice corporate law.

In fact, during my first year of law school, I felt such a strong calling to minister to women that I applied to the master's in biblical counseling program at Grace University, the institution where I completed my undergrad. I was only mildly crushed when I was rejected due to my speech impediment. I saw only two options when I received an inexplicable rejection in light of the fact that I was an alumnus currently attending law school on a full-ride scholarship after graduating from Grace summa cum laude just months prior.

One, I could sue Grace for blatant disability discrimination. As angry I was, I was only angry at the instructors of the master's program, not the undergrad program. As you will read later, I count my time at Grace as the best time of my life. I knew that suing Grace would not only result in damaging publicity but also likely bankrupt the entire college. Coverage of claims by insurance is never a given—especially for a tortious act that could likely be deemed intentional discrimination. When Grace shut its doors due to financial hardship just a few years later, my decision not to pursue legal action was affirmed in my mind. Further, Dad was a large donor and board member of Grace. I couldn't reckon with the fact that if I sued Grace, I could very well be taking money from his pocket.

This only left the second option—to take the rejection as a divine sign that God desired me to become an attorney. Although I still longed to take part in vocational women's ministry, I chose this option. I threw myself wholeheartedly into my studies. If I was going to endure the horrors of law school, I was going to make sure it was worthwhile. This meant earning the best possible grades to ensure I was employable despite my limitations. You already know the end: My efforts placed me in the top ten percent of my class following the fall semester. This in turn landed me the Union Pacific clerkship, which in turn landed me the associate position at a large law firm.

When I was rejected from the counseling program, I hoped that God might allow me to practice vocational ministry as an attorney. Yet when it came time for me to apply for postgraduation attorney positions, I couldn't find any positions in ministry.

The biggest hindrance was my inability to relocate. I require total care due to my cerebral palsy. This means that if my scheduled caregiver doesn't show up, I need to be able to call a family member or friend. In God's providence, he allowed 95 percent of my family to live in Omaha, Nebraska. Further, given that I have never lived anywhere other than Nebraska, most of my ride-or-die friends are here as well. This is a great blessing to me. However, it does hinder me from moving elsewhere for attorney ministry positions.

The second hindrance was that ministries often don't have a large budget for individual support staff. When I applied to private for-profit firms, I could bank on receiving at least some financial compensation for my disability-required assistant due to the almost universal use of secretaries by attorneys. However, this assumption wasn't as reliable when applying for nonprofit positions.

After being rejected from the counseling program and overwhelmed by limitations hindering my desired career in ministry, I wasn't over critical of my job offer from the law firm. I saw the offer, along with the promised assistance with paying my work assistant, as God's abundant provision.

I still see my associate position as God's abundant provision for a time. However, I'm overjoyed that, a short time ago, God paved the way for me to open my own law practice. As with most positive changes, the circumstances leading up to the changes weren't comfortable. My struggles at the law firm began almost from day one. Not only was the job utterly unfulfilling, but also, I had to fight tooth and nail for every little accommodation.

Nearing the end of my time with the firm, my physical health was at an all-time low. In one conversation with my brother shortly before resigning from the firm, he tried to encourage me by saying, "Maybe if you enjoyed your job, you would be able to work forty, maybe fifty hours a week again."

I laughed at the seemingly preposterous optimism, as at that time my cerebral palsy-related pain and fatigue was so high that even working three hours a day was simply unbearable. In frustration, I said, "You just don't get that cerebral palsy is a real thing in my life." The effects were real, but the permanent severity was not.

The fact of the matter was that, having little time to heal from law school before jumping into another proverbial fire, my mental state and emotions had worn thin. From day one at the firm, I knew this position would be an uphill battle. One of my good friends, Amber, agreed to be my work assistant when I started at the firm. She had so much confidence in me that she resigned from her previous position before we even knew whether I'd passed the bar exam—being the proactive overachiever I was, I wanted to start as an attorney a week after passing the exam. Given how close Amber and I were, I felt very confident when I stepped out of my car wearing my best suit and carrying a brand-new briefcase.

> One year ago, I was terribly sad that my faithful assistant of four years was graduating and going into the real world. Little did I know that I would get the opportunity to hire her back as my legal assistant just a year later. There will be many stresses that come with being a new attorney, but thankfully a good assistant won't be one of them. It also helps that we

are the best of friends and went through college and so much other life together. Once again, God is faithful.
—April 6, 2016

I think that Amber and I both had hopes of being a dynamic attorney-assistant duo like you see on TV. My high spirits were almost immediately brought crashing down to earth when I was greeted by a harsh-looking human resources director. True to my first impression of her, she would be a constant thorn in my side for the next four years. Before my first week was even over, she notified me that there were severe concerns about my wheelchair driving. This absolutely made me feel so welcome and comfortable at the firm—not. I think that was when I realized I would never fit in at this firm.

In all reality, it's a miracle that I persevered for almost four years in such a harsh and unforgiving environment considering that after the first day I had one of the biggest meltdowns of my life. Thankfully, I maintained my professional demeanor the entire day—throughout every awkward introductory conversation. Some of the attorneys were genuinely kind, but others seemed wholly unsure of how to interact with me, evident from their uncertain stares. Despite my ability to maintain composure at the firm, as soon as Kersten drove me home, the waterworks began. I made it to my apartment before I started convulsing with tears. By divine providence, my best friend Heather had to swing by my apartment at that precise moment. Poor Kersten, although also a close friend, she needed backup to deal with my unexpected breakdown. Heather comforting me as I sobbed on the toilet is one of the dearest images of our friendship over the years. In her wisdom, she said, "Well, just give it a try. You can always quit."

Give it a try, I did. God gave me the strength and fortitude to keep working day after day until He provided a way out. There were some good days—like when I had opportunities to work with a named partner of the firm who was the gentlest and most soft-spoken man I've ever met. I esteem him so highly that I truly believe that if we had worked in a small firm together, I would be honored to work under him as long as possible. Apart from this man, there was another seasoned partner who took me under his wing as often as possible. Him being a devout Catholic, we were able to relate on both a professional and a moral level.

These two men provided many moments of grace, propelling me forward amidst all the other hardships of the job. Still, as with most work environments, many colleagues made my life difficult, making me feel that I could never measure up no matter how hard I tried. Further, the work I was doing felt meaningless in the grand scheme of eternity. I wasn't helping clients who I cared about, but rather large corporations.

I bided my time by looking toward the future. About three months into my position, I began a new romantic relationship with a man who I anticipated marrying within a year or two, given our ages. Although he didn't treat me well, the fault of the relationship was not his alone, as I primarily simply desired to get married so that I could quit my job far more than I desired to marry him. When he ended the relationship almost a year later, I spiraled into a deep depression—not because I missed him, but because I missed the hope that I would soon be free from the job I detested.

Yet I didn't feel peace from God to resign at that time. So I marched on. The projects got worse. The human resources manager became more hostile. And I became number. Eventually, Amber wanted to pursue her own career ambitions—I couldn't blame her, given that the only aspect of the job we enjoyed was each other. I wouldn't want to spend my life taking dictation of meaningless corporate law briefs in an unfriendly environment either.

I applied for numerous other jobs throughout my time at the firm. I also tried to transfer to the estate planning department of the firm, hoping that working with individuals would provide more meaning to my work. Further, there was a clear glass ceiling to my career in litigation because my speech impediment prevented me from making court appearances and negotiations with opposing counsel. I believed that working one-on-one with individuals in planning for the future would afford me a career with no ceiling. However, every attempt was thwarted, met with adversity that couldn't be overcome no matter how hard I tried.

Ultimately, God provided a way for me to slowly transition into resigning from this unpleasant position. Though I didn't see it at the time, He used my physical pain and depression to lead me to go part-time with the firm. When I made the decision, I did so because I only wanted to hate life three and a half days a week. I thought that having Fridays off would make life bearable until I could retire. Unbeknownst to me, God wanted me to become accustomed to living on less money for when I started my own firm. Further, He wanted to force me to move from my ridiculously expensive apartment into a financially wise house that would be large enough to accommodate my law practice in its beginnings.

Following Amber, one of my most faithful caregivers, Anna, volunteered to help me at the firm while she took a year's sabbatical from school. I hoped that she might enjoy the job well enough to stay on long-term, but in reality, how could I expect her to find joy in a job too miserable for me to do full time? She was God's provision for a time.

Even still, God paved the way for me starting my own law practice when my firm unexpectedly moved me to work at home six months after Anna returned to school. At the time, my parents were discouraged for me, seeing this as an unfair setback in my career. I, on the other hand, was already so detached from the firm and any career aspirations that I once had that I couldn't have cared less as long as I was still getting a paycheck. In fact, not having to arrange transportation to and from the office every day was a welcomed relief.

When Anna returned to school, finding a new assistant proved to be extremely difficult. In desperation, I even tried to work at home without an assistant for several weeks. My valiant efforts at total independence were rewarded with crippling shoulder pain from trying to type everything on my own and countless additional hours spent on tasks that were previously completed in less than half the time.

Before Anna had agreed to be my work assistant, my cousin recommended that I ask the wife of the youth pastor at my church, Sharalee. My cousin, who is two years older than me, attended college with this young woman. Although I also attended the same college, I never knew Sharalee well while there. Ironically enough, she served as student body association treasurer immediately prior to my appointment to the same position. Even though I attended church with her, I didn't know her well enough to feel comfortable asking her to be my assistant at the time of my cousin's suggestion. In fact, falling into the tendency of making faulty assumptions about pastors' wives, the thought of working day in and day out under the constant scrutiny of a pastor's wife wasn't appealing to me in the least. I mean, I like to think that I live my life fairly consistently across the board, but I previously experienced a certain amount of judgment from a well-meaning Christian caregiver even just for listening to non-Christian music. I had no interest in repeating that scenario.

But desperate times call for desperate acts of faith. Even

though Amber and Anna had been literal godsends, not all my past work assistants had treated me well. One work assistant swore at me, stole jewelry and money from me, and yelled at me to the extent that it was even difficult to relax enough to use the bathroom with her aid. My thought in asking Sharalee to consider being my work assistant was simple: *She might be an annoying self-righteous pastor's wife, but it is only for a few days a week, and at least, I know she won't swear at or steal from me.*

Boy, my preconceived notions of her were wrong. By some miracle, she agreed to work for me after I sent her a pleading Facebook message. As typical, I was anxious about my first day with a new assistant. However, within the first few days, it became abundantly apparent that we were the dynamic duo that I'd always wanted. Eventually, with her help, I emerged from my great depression and became emotionally stable enough to make the riskiest decision of my life—starting my own law practice.

Over the months of working together, Sharalee gave me the confidence to begin recruiting clients. Although I was confident in my intellect, having confidence that clients would be receptive to my legal skills and abilities despite my cerebral palsy was difficult. This difficulty was magnified by the firm's confinement of me to the brief-writing box. Try as I might, to transition into the estate planning and corporate transaction department, the firm seemed unconvinced that I would be able to consistently bring in clients.

At the same time, years of stress were finally taking a toll on my body. Individuals with cerebral palsy frequently experience more fatigue than the average person. As happy as I was working with Sharalee, the stress of litigation work greatly exacerbated my fatigue. With no end in sight, my body all but shut down most days—unable to produce enough adrenaline to keep the machine going down an endless road.

In a final attempt to switch to the less stressful estate planning and corporate transaction department, I offered to bring multiple estate and corporate clients to the firm. The firm's response was astounding: "Thank you for the connections. We will take it from here." To say this was the last straw seems like an understatement. I was hit with another crippling wave of depression, even desiring to drive my wheelchair down my staircase just to get out of this unending situation.

Thankfully, unlike other bouts of depression, my mental and spiritual health were in a far more secure state. Additionally, given that I'd already been exiled to work at home for almost a year, my daily interactions were filled almost solely with people who loved and supported me. For example, Sharalee was a trusted godly woman to talk through my feelings and options with during the tumultuous week.

By now you should know that I never make big decisions without an exhaustively thought-through plan that has been vetted for months or years. If I ever opened my own law practice, I anticipated following the same Janae-certified protocol. Proverbs 16:9 says, "In their hearts humans plan their course, but the LORD establishes their steps." No truer words have ever been spoken. Within the span of a week, I decided to resign my position for disability reasons—a completely accurate statement in light of my inability to continue in the litigation department or secure another position in or outside of the firm. Humbling myself enough to apply for disability assistance, I ensured that I could continue to pay Sharalee, my other caregivers, and necessary living expenses. My natural aptitude for budgeting and finances had never been so critical.

Next, I cheerfully wrote my resignation letter to the firm. How long I'd imagined penning the words "Please accept this as my official and final resignation." It felt as if every ounce of job-induced stress left my body when I hit the Send button. Suddenly, the world was my oyster—juicy with hope and new possibilities, even if full of uncertainties. Even being on disability assistance, I knew I could perform a regulated amount of work without losing my eligibility.

Can't sit around forever, I thought. My parents also loudly echoed my sentiment. "No better time than now to hang my own shingle and see if I can achieve what the firm never gave me the opportunity to do—secure my own estate and corporate clients." A week later, COVID-19 shut America down.

As I sit here dictating this book to Sharalee, COVID-19 rages on. However, God has faithfully provided for us financially through disability assistance and clients. One might wonder if I regret resigning from a steady-paying job immediately before economic turmoil swept through the country. Without batting an eye, my answer is "not even remotely, not for one second."

Today, each workday, as my eyes flutter open around 9:00 a.m., a peaceful smile crosses my face as the light of a new day fills my view. As Rosie eagerly licks my face, I thank God for leading me to be my own boss. I roll out to my kitchen, where Sharalee's smile greets me with a cup of caffeine. We evaluate the agenda for the day—my level of fatigue, the household chores that can't wait, and any pressing volunteer or paid client matters. I open my email without dread, knowing that I answer to no one but God. This is work, true work. The type of work referred to in Genesis, created to bring us joy and purpose.

I wouldn't have this work if not for those twenty-two minutes at my birth—the ultimate moments of grace in my life that resulted in cerebral palsy, directing me to this dream job, perfectly suited for me.

Part Two

RELATIONSHIPS

Family Roots

Depicting the love of my family is not an easy task. Apart from God himself, my immediate family deserves much of the credit for my beautiful life. I have come to realize that if I could trade my CP-plagued life for a normal life, I wouldn't do so if the trade meant sacrificing any aspect of my family. We love each other. We don't just say it. We do it. Still, we probably say it more than any family I have ever heard. The courage of Dad gave me strength to dream. The compassion of Mom made me secure enough to thrive with joy. The kindness of my older brother made my awkward teen years bearable. The encouragement of my younger brother helped me maintain hope in my dreams. Finally, the selflessness of my little sister assured me that I'll never be left uncared for in this world.

> So overwhelmed by the blessing of a good family! I'd take life with cerebral palsy over life without a good family any day
>
> —May 14, 2018

Janae Hofer

The Courage of a Father

Dad's life could be summarized by the moments of his courage. He has chosen to live with courage in the face of insurmountable odds and adversity. He is a self-made man through and through. He would probably object to the self-made description and say instead that he is a God-made man. He would be correct.

He didn't come from an extraordinary background. My grandpa, who I love dearly, was a farmer-turned-insurance-salesman in Montana. When he gave up his thriving life insurance business to follow the majority of his children to Omaha, Nebraska, my grandfather never experienced the same level of success in his career. This sacrificial love for the sake of family inspires me. My grandmother was a hardworking housewife, who dedicated her days to tirelessly serving her family of seven. While their five children still lived at home in Montana, the family traveled and sang at churches. My grandfather was also a preacher.

Dad, the baby who didn't have a strong love of singing, sometimes felt lost amongst the voices of his three older sisters. When he attended Grace University in Omaha, Nebraska, he courageously decided to chart his own path. His initial plan was to become a shop teacher—a dream inspired by his own shop teacher who had mentored him. One of the main reasons he ended up at Grace University is because my grandfather promised to pay for college as long as he attended one year of Bible college. Yet Grace University didn't have a shop-teacher program.

By divine providence, Dad enjoyed Grace enough to come back a second year. This was the year he met the first and only love of his life—Mom. This was also the year that she broke his heart by dumping him after about six months of dating. She feared they were moving too fast. However, his unwavering kindness and relentless pursuit of her eventually won her back.

After searching the scriptures for every passage on how God called him to treat Mom even in the face of their painful breakup, Dad sat her down one more time and promised to treat her with the love and respect that a sister in Christ deserved. During their breakup, he also carved her a jewelry box, placing it in the gallery where she worked. Upon discovering this surprise, I would have sprinted back into the loving arms of my adoring ex-boyfriend. Mom is more logical than I. It took discovering that Dad was leaving for Africa for her to realize that she did indeed love him.

As a young twenty-one-year-old, my courageous father set out for Liberia completely on his own to perform maintenance and help build a hospital in a remote community. Mom stayed behind to continue her nursing training. After living in grass huts, transporting a decaying body for burial, and outsmarting corrupt officials who threatened to hold him hostage, Dad returned to the states—a few pounds lighter and a few proverbial decades wiser.

Shortly after his return, at the age of twenty-two, Dad proposed to Mom in a car full of her family while Christmas caroling. When Mom stated that her hands were cold, Dad offered to let her wear his warmer gloves. The engagement ring was hidden inside. Again, my reaction would have been to squeal to high heaven, loud enough for the whole county to hear. However, my more subdued mother whispered in Dad's ear: "Is this for real?" Upon hearing his reassuring response, she quietly, but excitedly, whispered yes. After carols, she waited to see how long it took her family to notice the ring. At this point, the squealing was finally brought into the equation. Apparently, my grandpa (Mom's dad) was caught off guard because Dad had only asked for his blessing a few hours earlier. Again, Dad doesn't lack courage.

After a typical farm-town wedding, my parents enjoyed a honeymoon in the mountains. Money was tight, so when Mom turned twenty-two a few days after their wedding, they celebrated

~ Janae Hofer ~

with a meal of canned soup cooked on the car engine while they camped beside the road. This adventurous spirit is one of the defining characteristics of their relationship and, by extension, my family.

The honeymoon led to Dad's first job after graduation—a youth pastor at a Presbyterian church in Omaha. Although he only served as a youth pastor for a few years, the congregation at the church eventually served as an instrumental support system following my birth. This position was in line with my parents' passion—ministry. Prior to my arrival, they planned to go overseas as missionaries.

However, following his stint as a youth pastor and facilitator at another ministry organization, Dad unknowingly hung up his vocational ministry cap for good. God had a different cap for him—one that would lead to the formation of multiple businesses, the gaining of much recognition, and lay ministry to thousands of people. Still, these events would be years down the road. When he transitioned out of full-time ministry, he was merely trying to faithfully follow God in a way that used his gifts and provide for his family. This initially meant hiring himself out for odd construction jobs. At one point, he spent days busting out concrete with a sledgehammer. Little did he know that he would become the premier builder of multimillion-dollar houses in Nebraska. His willingness to faithfully follow God and take risks for his dreams not only makes him one of the most courageous men I know, but has helped me have the courage to follow my own God-given dreams.

> This year I'm thankful for my dad for a new reason—
> He gave me the courage to start my new business
> because of his example of trusting and following God
> with his own business. Not going to lie, even though

he is loving and caring, we had a number of difficult discussions when I made the seemingly rash decision to resign from my position at a large law firm. "Simply not working is not an option. You can work less, but you too smart and gifted to give up your legal career." His confidence in me gave me the courage to try. His experience in business gives unfettered access to wisdom beyond my years. His commitment to never giving up gives me strength to do the same! I love you, Dad.

—June 21, 2020

He was still busting out concrete when I entered the scene. I imagine that for someone who was so fearlessly used to fixing problems, my birth must have been tremendously difficult. His joy at my arrival quickly turned to chaos at my first unsuccessful breath. To be sure, he instantaneously relied upon his faith as he quickly moved to Mom's side.

The minutes and hours, along with the months and years that followed, certainly tested his faith. Statistics indicate that fathers of severely handicapped children are immensely more likely to leave the home. He stayed. Not only did he stay, but also he was engaged with the entire family, including me. He gave us a comfortable life as God blessed his hard work, but he also gave us time. He was home for almost every evening meal. He was cheering at almost every school event. He was our youth group leader for a number of years. He was the driver on our annual two-week vacations. He was our rock and earthly hero.

> You provided for our family abundantly well. You built us a loving home. You built me a playhouse. You took me on wild ATV adventures. You took us to church every Sunday but modeled faith every

day of the week. You worked hard with excellence to build successful businesses but did not sacrifice family time to do so. You woke up at 4:30 a.m. so that you could be present for six-thirty family dinner, school events, weekends, holidays, and vacations. You were there when I needed you, but raised me to be strong and independent, challenging me to use my gifts and abilities for God's glory and to make a living for myself, assuring me that you will still be there to catch me if I fall. You remodeled my house with a hurting knee (pictured below), as just one example of how you support all my wild endeavors. Above all else, you love me unconditionally and continue to point me to Christ as my ultimate source of provision and security. I love you, Dad. Happy Father's Day.

—June 16, 2019

Today was an exciting day for my family. My dad is absolutely the humblest man I know, so he doesn't like drawing attention to his successes. But he has been planning this development since 2002. He kept going even when things became unbelievably difficult during the longest real estate recession in American history. Today his hard work and perseverance paid off. He broke ground for Avenue One in the presence of the governor, mayor, and other instrumental people in this project.

I know that young children often see their dads as superheroes. My dad still seems larger than life to me. I can't fathom how the same godly man who tucked me in every night, never missed family dinner or school events, drove us to church every week, and still picks up the phone every time I call—no matter how trivial the problem, has achieved this amount of success in

> one generation. It blows my mind that the same guy who had eight dollars in the bank when I was born worked hard enough to make his dream a reality. He attributes all of his success to the grace of God as my dad tried to be faithful. While I can't disagree, I still believe that my dad is the most amazing man I know and will ever meet. My mom may be my best friend, but my dad will always be my number one hero.
> —September 12, 2019

Specifically related to me, Dad fully embraced the challenge of raising a handicapped daughter. Dad is an extremely loving, but not cuddly, man. This meant that he didn't let me get away with anything. He was never going to play the violin in my pity party or let me off the hook because of my disability. He pushed me from day one and never stopped:

"You want water? Use your words."

"Smile and look people in the eye."

"Drive your wheelchair with your head up high."

"Do your best in school."

And so on.

> I love these two more than anything. I'm one of those blessed people who grew up with parents who said they were proud of me all the time. My dad would always say, "I'm proud of you, but not just because you achieve." I never understood how that could be because I'm a perfectionist overachiever. This past month, I feel like I finally understand because I'm struggling to measure up professionally, but for some reason, they are still just as proud and supportive as ever.
> —February 24, 2018

But for as much as Dad pushed me, he also showed me grace. Imagine the adjustments that this man's man had to undergo when he was handed a pink blanket with a severely disabled infant who would grow into a severely disabled child, adolescent, and adult. He dealt with my constant drooling in public. Further, until law school robbed me of belly-aching laughter and made my muscles permanently tighter, I wet my pants when I laughed too hard. On more than one occasion, I was out with Dad on one of our daddy-daughter dates when the cousin to Aunt Flow showed up, resulting in wet pants. One time, such a visit came when I was on stage at a talent show for a Girl Scouts' father-daughter banquet. I don't remember what Dad did, but my lack of memory shows that he handled the situation without permanently scarring his seven-year-old daughter.

We went on to have many more father-daughter dates, which usually involved shopping. Whether he realized it or not, he was unique even among the dads of severely handicapped children who stayed—because of shopping. I know this is a strange point to emphasize, but stick with me. Most parents of disabled children are worried about survival. Fashion and appearance are low on the list, if they even make the list. Contrarily, my parents saw fashion and appearance as a way to not only build my confidence, but also give me one more normalizing factor by which to relate to my peers. Dad's willingness to cultivate my femininity in this way, while still not spoiling me, was invaluable to my success in life as a whole.

> [Janae Hofer] just got the nicest pair of shoes she's ever had from her dad! Yes, I feel special! How often do I get to go out with just my dad and two brothers?
> —June 25, 2010

Lest Mom read the last sentence and throw this book against the wall, Mom actually deserves most of the credit for my fashion sense. Even though Dad gets credit for shopping outings every two years, Mom gets credit for finding the time and energy to do my hair and makeup, shave my legs, and dress me in clothes other than sweatpants. As you will see, this is especially commendable not only because I was one of four children within seven years of each other, but also because she grew up on a farm—where fashion wasn't exactly high on the totem pole.

But this section is about Dad, who should also be called my personal Mr. Fix-It. Not only can he figure out a way to fix almost anything, but also, he can create almost anything I need. When you are disabled, you need many items that have not been made or have not been made well enough to handle your muscle spasms. For example, many plastic phone and iPad holders exist, but in 2009, Dad made metal versions that will not break. After I destroyed a few wheelchair cup holders, Dad made a metal version of that as well. In addition, when my new wheelchair was two inches too wide to fit in my van, he took the wheelchair apart and figured out a way to make it two inches narrower. Keep in mind that power wheelchairs cost around $20,000, and by altering it himself, he voided all warranties. Despite all of the nail-biting and hand wringing that Mom and I did during the process, he was ultimately successful.

> Reason 956 why my dad is the best: He calls me in the middle of the workday asking the year of my car so he can get me new tires for winter. Of course, I didn't even think of doing that, because automobile maintenance is not among my competencies. #strongindependentwomanstillneedsdad
>
> —October 21, 2016

Not all of his inventions have been critically necessary. When we purchased a large acreage when I was seven, he tirelessly worked until 3:00 a.m. creating a frame for my wheelchair with bigger wheels. The intent was to allow me to drive all over the land. He was so excited that he woke me up when he finished and had me try it out in the dark. Although it broke down the next day, he is continually in search of the perfect outdoor wheelchair. The last time he presented me with an option, I proposed that he help me buy a new handicapped-accessible car instead. I'm sure he will try again now that I have that car.

Another one of his inventions was a cart that he and my brother used to pull me up a mountain. The big wheels were intended to make it easier to wheel me over boulders. The long pole handles extended both directions from the seat of the cart. They harnessed themselves to the poles, enabling them to pull and push me up the mountain trail. This was the same cart that Dad unsuccessfully tried to strap to the four-wheeler and pull me in. After a few flip overs, he decided to abandon the idea. I wasn't harmed physically or emotionally in any of these adventurous endeavors.

I don't know if I can say the same for Mom, especially when she nervously watched Dad use a battery-operated winch to pull me up into a hut built at the top of our windmill. Did I mention that I was pulled through a hole that was cut into the floor of the hut? Oh, and besides a harness, the only thing holding my weight was the duffel bag that I was pulled up in. Dad had dreams of me going hunting with him in that hut—he took me and my sister one time. Apparently, laughter and chatter scare the deer away.

Obviously, with all of these adventures, Dad had to have a sense of humor. Perhaps his humor is most exemplified in the following situation. When I was four, I habitually asked for water before bed. One night, he asked how many cups of water I wanted. Unfortunately for him, my favorite number at the time was eighteen. Naturally, I asked for eighteen cups of water. True to his word, he brought two trays in with eighteen cups of water and proceeded to give me a drink from each one until I died laughing.

It should be obvious by now that God knew what he was doing when he gave me Dad. As will be seen in the rest of this book, Dad has been present in many moments of grace beyond those described above.

The Compassion of a Mother

Trying to portray Mom in a matter of words seems like an insurmountable task. She's the person I need the most. I often wonder what I would do if I lost her. My mind refuses to go there, relying on the truth that God's grace would be sufficient even then. Still, I pray that if God doesn't provide me with a husband, he will take me home before Mom. Obviously, Mom hates it when I talk this way, but I simply can't imagine living in a world that she's not in. Mom is not only important, she's everything. She is God's greatest grace to me.

> Let me tell you about my mom: She's the one who made me doll clothes when we couldn't afford to buy them. She's the one who always made sure I was involved in every activity when I was a kid. When I didn't fit in during junior high or high school, I knew that things would be okay if I could just make it to 3:15 p.m. because her kind and loving face would greet me in the parking lot, and we'd go sip lemonade and chat. She is the one who never stops loving me even when I fail. She chooses to take joy in her lawyer of a daughter and not compare me to anyone else. She's the woman who raised me to love God and I'm so blessed.
> —May 8, 2016

She was no doubt terrified at my birth. But though she would have been in tears, she would have been composed. That's Mom—gracefully composed at all times, but somehow still genuine. The fact that she hadn't been coddled as a child gave her the stamina that she would need to be Mom. God picked her to raise me, equipping her with a nursing background to give her more confidence. But she would have risen to the challenge with no training at all if need be. She was strong enough.

In the months that followed my birth, she rotated taking care of my older brother and being at the hospital with me. When one parent was with one child, the other was with the opposite child. By God's grace, Dad's parents had just moved to Omaha, so my parents regularly left my brother in their capable hands. Mom had been working as a nurse up until my birth, which gave them enough insurance coverage to cover my initial hospital bills. Despite having been awarded nurse of the year on her floor after only beginning her career a few years prior, Mom gave up her career to be at home with me and my siblings.

Although she had intended to be an at-home mom, giving up her career meant losing the primary household income. Remember: at this time, Dad was busting out concrete and doing other odd jobs. Mom was content to live in a hundred-year-old farmhouse that housed chickens prior to housing my family. Determined to make this former chicken coop a home because it was only $200 a month rent, my parents found cost-efficient ways to fix up the two-bedroom, one-bathroom house. Apparently, the first year I was alive, we had to utilize government assistance to pay for my formula. This is because Dad only made $7,000 that year. My parents still found a way to donate $1,000 to church and mission work.

As a young child, I never knew we didn't have much money. Mom knew how to make our life good without spending much money, shopping at garage sales to buy us clothes and toys. At one garage sale, she found a year's worth of clothes for me for five dollars. They were all pink, so maybe that is why I'm still a girly girl who loves tasteful splashes of pink. One Christmas, she sewed a wardrobe of clothes for my doll. Every creative method she employed to give us a good life is etched in my memory.

I never felt safer than when I was in Mom's arms. Let me rephrase that. I still never feel safer than when I'm embraced by her loving arms. This is probably because she has always known me best. When I was around four years old, I was evaluated by a specialist who was unwilling to say that my cognitive function was age appropriate. Mom, who already knew I would get a doctorate someday, was infuriated. She turned to me and said, "Janae, if you have three apples and you get two more, how many apples do you have?" I answered five. Even though this wasn't enough to persuade the doctor to change his notes, it was an indication of Mom's unwavering confidence in me.

As I grew, so did her confidence in me. She let me try different activities even though I know she must have been so tired from taking care of four kids. One time, I wanted to bake. She gave me a little pan, allowing me to put four pepperonis and some flour in it. As a four-year-old, I thought this was the best recipe ever. Even though the finished product wasn't edible, she had allowed my creativity to blossom, which must have been one of her primary objectives throughout my entire childhood. She let me scribble on as much printer paper as I wanted, taping it to the counter so it wouldn't move. When I was in kindergarten, I started typing three-sentence stories with three words in each sentence: "Dog sat cat," "Mom got cat," and "Dad got mad." She got so excited about every story, printing it off and saving it.

As I got older, she paid me to write the *Hofer Herald*, which was a monthly newsletter about our family and my opinions on current events. The distribution list included friends and family. She did this not only to develop my writing skills, but also to teach me how to work. Given my physical limitations, everyone had to be creative with my chores. Mom and Gandma paid me 75 cents an hour to crawl along the baseboards and wipe them with a damp rag. I also retrieved the mail for everyone when the weather was nice. Although I dropped some letters on the way because of my clumsy hands, no mail was ever lost. The situation was without exception rectified in the end.

In the educational scene, Mom was without a doubt my advocate. She made sure I was receiving the same quality of education as everyone else. She accompanied me to every meeting about my accommodations all the way until I was accepted into law school. At that time, we both made the unspoken decision that it was time to cut the cord. I knew she would still be there if I needed her.

I think that knowing when to push me to be independent might have been the hardest part of raising me. For example, up until college, only she, my grandmas, and my aunts had ever assisted me with personal care. However, Mom knew that it was critical for me to live in the dorms and be assisted by paid caregivers. In faith, she left me crying in my dorm on the first day of college after handing me the keys to a minivan that I would never drive. (The idea was to have my future friends drive.)

This step of faith was critical for me to grow independent enough to move to an apartment with a roommate after college, then an apartment with no roommate after law school, and then my very own house. Although I used to get upset with her sometimes for not being more empathetic about my disability, imagine where I would be if I'd have had a mother who coddled me and allowed me to engage in self-pity. I'll tell you. I would be a thirty-year-old unemployed disabled woman living in my parents' house. My pool of friends would be significantly smaller because I would have never pushed myself to build relationships. And I wouldn't be writing this book.

Just because Mom didn't coddle me doesn't mean she didn't let me cry. Perhaps the most searing memory of her compassion for me is from a Girl Scout retreat. Later in this book, you will read about my seven-year battle with rejection by my former group of school friends. I call these friends the "Girls." At this particular Girl Scout retreat, the Girls decided that they all wanted to sleep on the top bunks, regardless of the fact that I was on a bottom bunk. Mom, not wanting me to be left out, managed to deadlift my eleven-year-old body onto a top bunk.

Annoyed that their plan to exclude me had been foiled, the Girls proceeded to move to the top bunks on the other side of the room. My sweet mom quietly walked over to me, gently stroked my hair, wiped my tear-filled eyes, and said, "Janae, I can't move you again, but you know that I love you. Your family loves you and God loves you. Don't let them get to you." Looking back now, I would have rather gone through that with Mom by my side than fit in with the best of the Girls.

This single moment solidified my entire future relationship with Mom. From that day on, she was my best friend. She was the one I looked forward to seeing after school, knowing that, no matter what happened at school, everything would be okay as soon as I saw her smiling face waiting for me in the car. We drove home and had snacks as we chatted about my day. I didn't begin struggling with depression until college partially because, when I was living with her, she knew how to make my darkest days bright. She either watched a movie with me, called my aunts and cousins to come over, or simply read to me on the porch for hours. Even though she probably knew I would never fit in with the Girls again, she took me shopping for cute clothes, learning how to do my hair and makeup in the trendy ways. When it came time for prom, she overcame her frugal roots and bought me the prom dress of my dreams. It was pink, of course.

Mom has made countless other sacrifices for me. Most of them involved selfless hours of service. When I was in high school, my friends were from an Omaha church that my family attended. Since we lived in a small town ten miles outside of Omaha, she regularly drove me into Omaha to meet these precious friends. She knew how life-giving they were to me. Beyond driving me places, she spent countless hours writing my math homework for me—all the way through senior year. Although by the time I was in elementary my family likely had enough money to hire a caregiver for me, she only hired a nanny once for a summer after my baby sister was born—when she had a newborn and three other children seven and under. Even at that, the nanny only came about three days a week. No one would have faulted her for hiring more help for me, but she wanted to keep family life as normal as possible.

This meant that, until I moved to college, she was my sole caregiver, responsible for dressing, feeding, and bathing me 24/7, 365 days a year. Also, I didn't figure out how to get out of bed on my own until I was much older. If I ever needed to use the bathroom or have a drink of water in the middle of the night, I had to wake her. As a child, I didn't have the mature insight to realize how tired Mom must have been at the end of each day. Had I known, I would have likely gone many more nights without a drink of water or a trip to the bathroom.

When I moved to college, Mom took a break from being a regularly scheduled caregiver for about eight years with the exception of holidays, summer vacations, and emergency fill-in shifts. This was healthy for both of us. For me, who would cry if I had to go without seeing her for more than four days, I needed to develop independence and my own identity. I needed to learn to be comfortable with other people caring for me. I also needed to learn to rely on others for emotional support. For her, she too needed to learn to be independent from me. She needed to focus more on my younger siblings for a while. She needed to enjoy some more freedom for herself.

Note that I didn't say that she needed some time off. There was no real time off. Given that my college and law school were only a twenty-five-minute drive from home, she was perpetually on call if I needed anything. We were so close that we usually saw each other at least once a week. Until recent years, we attended the same church, which led to continuing the cherished tradition of Sunday lunches out. When I was clawing my way through law school, she filled my freezer with frozen meals. As shocking as it may be, as a severely disabled law student, I had no ability to cook. Time with caregivers was strictly reserved for personal hygiene and dictating notes.

As I grew older, I found myself needing more and more of Mom's advice on my career, life, and depression battles. As a more logical and less emotional woman than I, she had to work extra hard to learn when to be sympathetic to my emotional breakdowns and when to challenge me to put on my big-girl pants so I could keep moving forward. The fact that we're still close shows that she found a sufficient balance even if imperfect. Had she been any more sympathetic, I would likely be a wimp. Had she shown any more tough love in her comments to me, I likely wouldn't still confide in her and cherish every moment with her as I do now.

> When you text your mom that you are feeling claustrophobic because you can't just hop on a plane and travel alone, and she proposes planning a trip together. 😍♡ How did I get the perfect mom?
> —May 21, 2019

The pages of the rest of my story will reveal that Mom is my greatest cheerleader. But more than trying to navigate my disability-inflicted life together, we simply have fun most of the time. She is my favorite shopping buddy because she gives me her honest opinion and finds the best deals. She is the best travel companion because we enjoy the same activities, hotels, and eating schedules. My favorite trip to date is when we went Dutch on a trip to Maine in 2017. However, who knows how long this will be my favorite trip because we intend to go on many more. She is the best example of a humble, genuine, godly woman, rising early to read her Bible after her morning workout and never failing to point me back to God's truth. Mom is not only important—she's everything.

The Kindness of an Older Brother

My older brother, Jamison, was almost two when I made my dramatic entrance into the family. Going against what one might assume, I've never felt any resentment from him for me stealing attention in those early years. This is probably partly due to my parents, but also due to Jamison's genuinely kind demeanor. Even at an early age, he tried to make me laugh. Before I was even two, he put Pringles in his mouth to form a duck beak simply to put a smile on my face.

As we got older, Jamison made sure I was included in all of the child's play possible. He helped me on the trampoline. He particularly loved helping me play in the mud. When this happened, Mom would end up spraying me off with a cold, garden hose. However, as frustrated as she seemed to be about having to clean up yet another mess, I'm sure that it gave her a certain amount of joy to see her older child include his younger disabled sister in the activities of young country life. As I look back now, I'm so grateful that Jamison wasn't too afraid of hurting me to play with me.

Jamison was never mean to me. At most, he held my arm to keep me from hitting at him when we were young children. I'm sure this was because Dad had made it clear that if either of my brothers ever hit me or my sister, they would answer to him. Still, Jamison wasn't afraid to play pranks on me. One time he turned the electric blanket on my bed at my grandma's all the way up to the highest temperature before I got in, causing me to sweat profusely until I finally called for help. Another time, he put our pet hamster in my bed, resulting in me squealing to high heaven. And too many times to count, he hid under my desk or around the corner in my bedroom to scare me. Because of my continual muscle spasms, even if I knew he was there, I still jumped when he "surprised" me.

Even with all his teasing, I never once doubted Jamison's love for me. This is probably because he never failed to put my needs first and defended me whenever necessary. When I was around ten, and he was around twelve, two female chaperones volunteered to take Jamison and four other adolescents to an amusement park. For some reason, Mom was unable to go, and no amount of crying on my part could persuade them to take me anyway. First, Jamison volunteered to carry me onto the rides and feed me, meaning that the only thing these chaperones who had previously cared for me would need to do was help me in the bathroom. Jamison's selflessness wasn't enough to convince them. They still said it was just too much work. So Jamison refused to go without me. I have never heard of a more selfless act from such a young teenage boy.

As we became teenagers, I felt more competitive with him. He not only got better grades than me, but also, he was a decent athlete. This meant that I spent many Saturdays at wrestling meets. I wish I could say that I unwaveringly played the role of the supportive sister, but many times I had an attitude about going. My attitude wasn't so much about not wanting to watch Jamison, but more about not wanting to have to spend another day not fitting in. You see, at wrestling meets, there were not only cheerleaders but also managers who were my female peers. Even if they had wanted me to interact with them, which they didn't, doing so was nearly physically impossible. Because of the crowds, I either had to sit in my wheelchair at the end of the bleachers, unable to follow the Girls around, or I had to sit in the bleachers with my parents. Given how difficult it was to carry me up the bleachers, it was necessary for me to stay in the same spot all day except for bathroom breaks.

My inability to interact with my peers, along with the unpleasantness of seeing girls being able to so easily flirt with the wrestlers when I was unable to do likewise, put a distaste for wrestling in my mouth. Unfortunately, I was too immature to adequately express my feelings. As a result, my feelings came out as a total disinterest in Jamison's wrestling career. Hopefully, my family realized that I wasn't totally disinterested when I literally jumped off the bleachers when he made it to state wrestling. Naturally, I ended up falling. It was worth it.

My competitive feelings toward Jamison extended to academics as well. We were in the same year in Spanish. He consistently earned better grades than me. However, I earned a better grade on one test. Boy, did I rub it in. He must have had endless compassion for me because he let me have the glory. He could have silenced me with the fact that he still had a higher overall grade, but he just humbly congratulated me.

He was also one of the most popular guys in school by the time he was a senior. His genuine kindness led people to elect him prom king and Mr. Calhoun. Yet he still made it clear that he valued me over anyone at school. Right after he was crowned prom king, he took a picture with me. He also drove me to every church event, allowing me to blabber on about whatever was on my mind. All of these little acts of kindness led to me bawling when we dropped him off at college in Arkansas. He was comforting, even though I know that having a disabled sister bawling in his freshman dorm room must have embarrassed him.

Even though I was sad about him attending college out of state, by God's grace Jamison found a wife from Omaha. He met Laura at church and was captivated by her contagious joy. Conveniently, they started dating right around the time Laura and I began our freshman year at Grace University. Divine providence allowed Laura and I to live on the same dorm floor, making my transition into college much more comfortable. She was my first of many new friends at college, but she's the only one who eventually became my sister. Through the years, she has proved to be selfless herself. Beyond supporting Jamison through med school and residency while birthing and raising four children, she also finds time to help me. She had me over for a weekend to their apartment in Des Moines when Jamison was gone—it was on the third floor of the building with no elevator so she carried me on her back. Since then, she has taken it upon herself to make sure my hair and makeup look nice for family pictures, finding time to style me despite having small children of her own.

The Encouragement of a Younger Brother

When I was two years old, my brother Jeffrey was born. Jeffrey is by far the most naturally intelligent of us all. Not only did he graduate Salutatorian from high school, but he was helping me with my eleventh-grade chemistry homework when he was in eighth grade. As a side note, the only reason he wasn't valedictorian was that his ninth-grade English teacher refused to round his 93.8 percent B+ up to a 94 percent A. He will probably be irritated that I mentioned that, but I'm a big sister, so it's my prerogative to brag.

Not only is Jeffrey highly intelligent, but he is sensitive in the way of emotional intelligence. He is as tough as any other man's man, but when the women he loves are hurting, he knows what to say. By women, I mean his mother, sisters, and wife. His daughters will eventually benefit from this emotional sensitivity as well.

One example of this emotional sensitivity is from homecoming my senior year. From fifth grade to graduation, a group of girls (the Girls) at my high school didn't particularly like me. The Girls received accolades for their academics and "niceness" to everyone. It's true that they were relatively nice on the surface, but they were not kind to or inclusive of me. As you will see in my chapter about friends, I didn't have the good judgment to just cease interaction with them rather than be continually hurt and disappointed.

A couple of days before homecoming my senior year, when I found out that one of the Girls was wearing the football jersey of my ninth-grade brother for homecoming, I became instantly emotional—beginning to cry. Poor Jeffrey was just being nice to the Girl, having no idea that her wearing his jersey would upset me so much. Not wanting to sound petty, the best solution I came up with in the moment was to insist that I wanted to wear his jersey. This was true. I did want to wear it. I'd just not thought about it until that moment. Despite his confusion about why I hadn't asked earlier, being the sweet younger brother that he is, it didn't take much to convince him. He informed the Girl that I would wear his jersey, and that was that.

Most of Jeffrey's kind encouragement came naturally during my difficult times. I have always struggled with the fact that my cerebral palsy hinders me from being attractive to many men. As a result, I often doubted whether I would marry. Jeffrey wouldn't allow me to ruminate on these negative thoughts. He instead made little comments like "Well, you'll be married too," "Your husband will help you with that," and "You'll get married. You're attractive." These comments helped keep my hope in finding love alive.

> I have the sweetest little brother. Driving down the road, he bangs the wheel and says, "Oh my goodness Janae, not true, you're very attractive, and you're gonna get married, have two kids, and make $100,000 a year!" It almost made me cry!
> —June 12, 2011

As he got older, Jeffrey took on more of the responsibilities for helping me out. I think the event that triggered this acceptance of responsibility was my panic-induced suicide attempt during my first year of law school. As you will read, law school was the worst time in my life. After being rushed to the ICU by a couple of friends, Jeffrey visited me. I was too ashamed to look my little brother in the eyes. I was his big sister. I was supposed to be an example, not a disaster. When I did glance at his eyes, I saw deep worry. He promised that I would be taken care of even when Mom and Dad died. It was a simple promise to say, but the implications were much more difficult.

As what I believe was a direct result of the promise, there was a shift in our relationship from that point on. Jeffrey picks up whenever I call, even if he's working. He flew in from Detroit to help remodel my house. I'm sure he would help me with anything and have a good attitude. One time when my sink was leaking, he stopped by before work to fix it. He leaves me no reason to complain about not having a husband to fix things, because all I have to do is ask. Of course, for as long as Dad is able, Dad wishes to bear the majority of these responsibilities. However, it brings me so much peace to know that Jeffrey is ready and able to step up to the plate when the time comes.

Following in Dad's and Jamison's footsteps, Jeffrey also found a good wife and married young. His wife, Maddie, is similar to me in her demeanor, fashion, and perfectionistic tendencies. She's also one of the sweetest people I have ever met. Like Jeffrey, she helps anyone she can. I was nervous to meet her because all I knew about her was that she was a gorgeous, intelligent, and a college athlete. However, her kind spirit eased my intimidation. I knew she was a keeper when she fearlessly fed me the messiest bean burrito in a moving car. I feel so fortunate to have two sisters-in-law who I know would take care of me. God provided. He always does.

The Selflessness of a Sister

No matter how great my brothers were, I wanted a baby sister more than anything. When I was five, my parents told us that Mom was pregnant with a girl. "Thank you, Jesus!" was my response. I was beyond thrilled to have someone to play Barbies and house with. Julie has brought so much joy and creativity into our family.

Of all my siblings, my cerebral palsy was the hardest on Julie, yet she chose to love me anyway. I admire her so much for this. Whereas my brothers seemed to adjust to life with a disabled sibling quite easily, it took a toll on Julie. Youngest children commonly feel overshadowed, but this feeling is probably magnified by one hundred when an older sibling has a severe disability. My parents tried to give Julie the attention she needed, but even during her youngest years, my disability demanded much attention. If Mom would be cuddling with Julie on the couch, but I needed to go to the bathroom, Mom would have to leave Julie to help me.

As a young child, this is difficult to process without allowing lies to sink in. She struggled with lies that everyone loved me more well into her twenties. No one can fault her for struggling, considering all of the time that Mom had to spend with me. Mom got me ready every morning, fed me every meal, helped me with homework every afternoon, and assisted me with bedtime every evening. Further, because I have slow speech, to a young child it would seem that I was talking to Mom more than my allotted time in a family of four children. All of these factors combined to make my disability more difficult for Julie.

When you are disabled, people make huge deals out of your smallest accomplishments. Sometimes I feel that all I would need to do was get out of bed with a smile on my face, and I would be someone's inspiration. Although I recognized the shallowness of such admiration early on, to Julie, who was five years my junior, it seemed that people were constantly giving me undue praise and attention. Eventually, after recognizing Julie's pain, this overwhelmed me with grief. It made me cringe that when Julie won speech awards, people were more prone to talk about my success in law school. It made me cringe that at her high school graduation reception, I had to worry about people wanting to hear about my academic endeavors. And it made me cringe that she felt less loved by my grandmas simply because they were more worried about me given my unique challenges.

> Happy birthday to my amazing, beautiful, creative hilarious sister! Thanks for always being willing to help me out. I don't know what I would do without you! It makes me tear up just thinking about it. You always tell me what I need to hear and cheer me up when I'm down. I love you more!
> —May 24, 2019

But, as hard as it was and is for her, Julie chooses to love me. We would not only say, "Good night! I love you" each night before we went to sleep in the room that we shared, but also, she would show her love. One time we were at a wedding with a dance. My high school crush was present. Julie loved me so much that I had to convince her not to ask him to dance with me. Another time, when I was a senior and she was a seventh-grader, the Girls had made me cry yet again. Julie bravely left a note in one of their lockers, asking the girl to please not be mean to me. Wow! What courage!

My younger sister's loving acts have continued over the years. Whenever I have a bout of depression, she supplies me with all the junk food I could ever want. Along those same lines, she's always there to comfort me whenever I cry, even if she has to do so over FaceTime because she's in another state.

One particular night I was caught off guard by how much I depend on her. She was the first one on the scene after the events described in the following Facebook post:

> Last night I experienced the scariest mishap of my life. Although my bed is against the wall to minimize the risk of falling, I got wedged between the wall and the bed when I tried to pick something up that had fallen back there. Thankfully, I was able to pull my head and upper torso onto the bed, but gravity pulled my legs down, trapping them between the metal frame and the wall. My initial squirming resulted in my legs getting twisted underneath the bed while still being pinched in a way that cut off circulation to my left leg. Try as I might, even allowing an unused internet jack to dig into my right ankle as I attempted to push up off it, I couldn't free myself.

In the three hours that followed, as I struggled in pain, I feared that the loss of circulation would cause the loss of my leg. Tears ran down my face. Sweat soaked my hair and clothes. The pain was unbearable. Even as my mind began to fail me, instead of questioning God as I would in the past, I found a certain amount of peace in trusting His sovereign plan as I recited scripture and hymns while still pleading with Him to send someone to help. During these dark moments, I was able to fully appreciate the extent that I have been freed from years of depression that haunted me until a few months ago because I sincerely did not want to die.

I would scream at the top of my lungs and bang the wall intermittently through the hours. My neighbor above me heard and eventually called the fire department, who broke in my door. Even after they moved my wheelchair so that they could pull the bed away from the wall and lift me onto it, my body shook. My mind was unclear from dehydration, pain, and fear. I was coherent enough to direct them to call Mom, but as I talked to Mom on the phone, she was shocked that her attorney-daughter was only verbalizing grunts. My sister beat my parents to my apartment, and found me half crying and only responding coherently to simple, direct questions.

As time went on, they calmed me down. Although I'm fine now, my legs are ankles are severely bruised with some surface cuts. We are looking into new safety measures, but as with everyone who even gets on the highway, we must ultimately continue to trust God for protection. Please pray for my speedy recovery, physically and emotionally, as it was quite traumatic for me mentally.

—November 4, 2018

This is Julie. Always there in my most painful moments when I need her the most.

The Extended Love

Beyond my immediate family, God has blessed me with amazing grandparents. As I sit here writing this, I feel unbelievably blessed that my four grandparents are all alive. I have lost all of my great grandparents, including great-grandmothers who fervently prayed for me. My favorite memory of a great-grandparent is of my Great-Grandma Harder. Whenever we visited Mountain Lake, Minnesota, where Mom's family lives, we went see Great-Grandma Harder in the nursing home. She was a serious but loving woman who had a sense of humor. I loved her so much that every time we left her room, I cried. She lived to be a hundred, passing away when I was finishing the seventh grade.

Mom's parents also live in a small Minnesota farm town. I have the best memories of my grandma throwing tea parties for us. My grandma is not only extremely loving, but a jokester. I don't remember how the bit began, but somewhere along the way whenever I told her I had to go to the bathroom she responded with one of the following phrases: "No! You already went today!" Or "No! You have to wait until tomorrow!" We have continued this exchange all the way to the present day.

Grandma also had us up to the farm to stay for days at a time. She worked extremely hard to keep us fed and entertained. She did all of this without the help of Mom on some occasions. One year particularly tested her limits as not only did she take us to the town festival on her own, but I also got the second period of my life that week. I was mortified and absolutely no help with resolving the issue, but she and my aunts managed to take care of the unfortunate situation, without having a breakdown themselves. Moreover, she entertained me for hours by playing Rummikub and dominos with me. My love for visiting her is shown by the fact that when I was devastated about a relationship ending my sophomore year of college, I went and stayed with her for a long weekend. Even then, she was able to take care of me on her own, making me strawberry pie (my favorite) and taking me to a local play. What a precious glimpse of the golden thread during such a difficult time.

I know that Mom's dad also loves me dearly. He is a gentle, quiet man who has worked hard for his family. His tender gentleness is seen when his voice cracks with emotion every time he prays or reads the Christmas story. My favorite memory of him is from when I stayed with them during my sophomore year of college. Even though it is difficult for him to understand me, he sat down in the quiet of the kitchen and fed me a bowl of ice cream. This was him showing me that he cared in a way other than the usual big kisses on my cheek. Further, he has made sure that he and my grandma were present at every important event in my life. Most special was to see them at my swearing-in ceremony as I became a licensed attorney in the state capitol.

Dad's parents are equally as important in my life. We got to see them almost daily when we were growing up because Dad sold them ten acres of our land, enabling us to be neighbors. This was a great help for my parents in the form of free babysitting. To prioritize their marriage, my parents would go away for about three to four days each year. During that time, my grandparents would stay with us. Not only did my grandma have to keep up with four energetic children, but she also had to take care of one with severe special needs. She did so flawlessly without batting an eye. Apparently, caring for me came so naturally to her that she volunteered to take me on a two-week trip to Brazil to visit my cousin. I was in between my junior and senior year of high school at the time, meaning that I wasn't small, and she wasn't young. Yet we braved a thirteen-hour nonstop flight to go to a country that wasn't exactly handicapped accessible.

Given that I'd been instant messaging and Skyping my cousin for years, I was thrilled to finally see where she lived. She was a person who made me feel loved during those difficult years with the Girls. I came home and talked to her about my day, and we laughed at the immaturity of adolescent girls. When her family came back to the states to visit, they stayed with my grandparents. I was thrilled to be within walking distance of my dear cousin. I could tell that she genuinely loved me because not only did she put up with my random babblings, but also she spent as much time with me as possible for an introvert who loved to read every waking hour. Yes, those months when they stayed with my grandparents glow in my memory.

As I got older, my grandma became more and more of a friend. Unable to drive anything but my wheelchair, my only avenue of escape as a teenager was to drive my wheelchair down the road to visit my grandma. I sat and talked to her as she sewed for hours. She gave me advice about matters of faith and the heart. And like any good grandma, she fed me goodies. Her sewing skills were so phenomenal that to this day she can mend any article of clothing I need. And she would take a break from sewing to play Scrabble with me.

My grandpa provides humor in my life. One time when I was eight, Dad was praying for family dinner. My grandpa poked me in the side, not realizing that I would jump so hard that my arm would clear all water glasses from the table in one fell swoop.

Dad opened his eyes and said, "What happened?"

My grandpa laughed so hard, and to this day still says, "What happened?"

Not wanting me to miss out on anything, there were a few times where he let me get into the hot tub with my clothes on because neither Mom nor my grandma was around to help me change into my swimsuit. Of course, they had to deal with the aftermath of this fun decision. His joyful spirit made it so fun to visit him as he worked in our shop.

Sometimes he worked with a cat on his shoulder. Whenever I visited him, he gave me a pop from the shop fridge. All I had to do was bring a straw from the house. We talked about random subjects, but he never failed to shower me with adoring compliments: "You are my miracle," "You are so beautiful—look at those eyes and that smile," "You are my angel," and "I don't know how in the world you live so joyfully. If I had to deal with what you live with, I would be miserable." He also prayed over me: "Heavenly Father, thank you so much for this beautiful girl. Help her body and mind to work well for your glory." His love is invaluable to me.

≈

Dad is one of five. Mom is one of seven. This means that I have a number of aunts. Many have been instrumental in encouraging my writing endeavors. Further, my aunts have sacrificially served me from the day I was born. I have many girl cousins around my age, which naturally meant sleepovers. Somehow, my aunts figured out how to get me up and down stairs for these coveted sleepovers all the way until we stopped having them when I was a sophomore in high school. As if they knew when Mom needed a brief break from caring for me, they handled all of the dressing and feeding of me while I was at their houses. Most of the time

Mom was at my grandma's during these get-togethers. Let's not forget how much laughter goes on at sleepovers, and thus how many times my aunts had had to change my wet pants.\

On that note, one time my aunt took me on an amusement park ride, which resulted in me laughing so hard that I wet my pants. Because we were in the same bench seat of the Tilt-A-Whirl, when my poor aunt stood up, her pants were also wet. Somehow, she still loves me.

Even apart from my cousins, my aunts invested in me. Growing up, I was particularly close to one aunt who took me on shopping outings followed by sleepover movie nights at her house when I struggled in junior high. She, too, figured out a way to get me up and down her stairs despite having back problems. She also never ceases to text and pray for me during hard or important times. We're also kindred spirits because of our love for fur fashion, decorating, pets, hotels, and nice restaurants. In fact, she, Mom, and I have an ongoing joke that I should have been born into her family instead of my outdoor, camping-loving family. I have no idea what would cause Mom to frequently call me her name by mistake.

Another aunt became an integral part of my life when I suffered from depression from age nineteen to twenty-six. As someone with a master's in counseling, she could often speak to me in a way that Mom could not. When I was in the ICU from the panic-induced ibuprofen overdose, I vividly remember her sitting by my bedside, holding my hand, and assisting Mom in deadlifting me onto the commode so that I could pass the charcoal that soaked up the excess ibuprofen. An aunt who sees you in a sweaty, noncoherent state of depression in the ICU, and still believes in you is irreplaceable. I can't fathom why she would still have the confidence to say, without blinking an eye, in her matter-of-fact voice, "Janae, you will write many, many more books. You have the heart and passion of a writer." I guess she must understand God's grace.

Even though they live miles away, my aunts in Minnesota continually invest in me. One example is a particularly frugal aunt who puts aside her frugalness enough to send me care packages. The most impressive care package was the congratulations-on-the-new-arrival care package that came when I adopted my beloved puppy, Rosie. Mind you, she hates indoor pets, but she knows how to show her single niece love—by buying all the cute dog products that probably make her roll her eyes.

In addition to my aunts, I have eleven girl cousins within five years of me. These cousins have loved me well. I think they all knew that I had trouble fitting in at school, so they always welcomed me with open arms. They didn't sign up to be bound to a severely disabled cousin, so the fact that they interacted with me in a way that made me feel loved is admirable. I wonder if it was ever hard for them. If it was, they never showed it. For my sweet sixteen birthday all of my Minnesota cousins came down for a sleepover and scavenger hunt at the mall. Again, the same aunts who took care of me helped plan the whole party. This is just one of the amazing memories I have of my Minnesota cousins. Another time, we all went to the Mall of America and tried on prom dresses just for fun. Mom even tried one on!

So many moments of grace involve my cousins. The older ones babysat me when I was young. I had the opportunity to attend college with four of my girl cousins. Perhaps the best evidence of how important they are to me is the fact that they have been present at many of the most important moments of my life. Just one example is the day when my cousin, who cared for me many times throughout the years, was with me when I received my bar exam results.

When I saw the email that would determine my future pop

up on my phone screen, my eyes went blurry, and I made excited noises and motions, indicating to her that the results that we had been expecting all morning had finally arrived at 11:05 a.m. Thankfully, she knew me well enough to realize that she was going to have to take my phone and read them herself before I started hyperventilating. My stomach tied into a sickening knot. She scrolled down the email as she read in a tear-choked voice, "We would like to congratulate you on passing the Nebraska State Bar Exam."

At that point, we both teared up as I exclaimed, "I'm an attorney!" We proceeded to rejoice as we called and texted all who were eagerly awaiting the news.

⁓

Hopefully, now it is clear why I would choose my family over a life free from cerebral palsy. My family made my cerebral palsy not only bearable, but truly enjoyable and humorous at some points. We learned how to live with the disability together. In some ways, the disability made our bond stronger as I contrasted the rejection from the outside world with the love I felt from my family. Moments with my family, good or bad, are moments of grace because they are moments of sacrificial love.

Finding Friends

Moments with my friends are among the most cherished, grace-apparent flickers in my life. It took me awhile to find my life-giving friends, but it also took me a while to refine the art of being a good friend in light of my cerebral palsy. How can I ever give them as much as they give me when they must feed me, assist me in the bathroom, and patiently wait for me to finish my slowly spoken sentences that require focus to understand? Why would they want to make the sacrificial effort to be my friend?

To be sure, many people have chosen not to make the effort. However, I count myself as abundantly blessed because my friends are the rarest of diamonds, reflecting life's shared flickers in the most breathtakingly beautiful display of love. In return, they have again and again assured me that I give more than I take, reminding me of the steadfast love and commitment I give as well.

The journey to find these diamonds, and to learn how to continually discover new gems, wasn't easy. It was painful and messy, much like the way miners are required to dig through soot and rock just to find these rare treasures. At times, when the heat, tears, and messiness were most intense, the task seemed futile in the dark mines of youth. Was I even searching in the right cave? Would my disability forever prevent me from mining genuine relationships?

No. God had a plan. Even in these dark and lonely times of searching, seemingly only warmed by joyful flickers of moments with my family, God's grace extended to the realm of friendships. In his sovereign grace, he needed to teach me the value and rareness of diamond friendships so that I would care and treasure them appropriately.

The first time I realized that friendship would be harder for me to come by was at the age of three or four in Sunday School. Two classmates didn't want to play with me because I "drooled and talked like a baby." Thankfully, when I began kindergarten, I made friends relatively easy. However, much like the jewelry you allow a five-year-old to wear, these first friendships weren't rare diamonds, but merely temporary placeholders for future gems. I'm so thankful for these placeholders. These placeholders allowed me to experience recess fun, sleepovers, and a relatively normal elementary experience in terms of friendships. I'm also thankful for the mothers who invited me to birthday parties and even assisted me with my personal needs at sleepovers. Regardless of the amount of coaching that Mom had to give prior to the sleepovers, the selflessness of the mothers of these girls in inviting me despite the physical demands is admirable.

For some girls, the jewelry they receive when they are young turns out to be genuine gems or priceless metals. The same can be said of early childhood friendships. Some childhood friendships stand the test of time, proving to be genuine and valuable. But most girls grow up to realize that the jewelry given to them as children will not stand the test of time because it is not made of genuine material. If these girls are fortunate enough, they will grow into women who will later acquire genuine jewelry.

≈

The faux childhood gems symbolize my early elementary friends well. Our friendship, made from the plastic beads of youth and bound together by nothing more than similar childhood interests, would not survive the harshness of adolescent life or beyond. Common childhood interests of Barbies and elementary crushes would fray, causing nothing but a hollow sound to resonate as the plastic beads slid off the frayed string and hit the floor. As I grew, so did the challenges of my disability—challenges too heavy for childhood jewelry to hold, and too heated for cubic zirconia to withstand.

In fifth grade, I began watching my childhood friendships crumble. The girls were still nice but didn't include me. Also, at this point, their academic performance far exceeded mine. As detailed in the "Educational Endeavors" part of this book, a number of factors hindered my academic success in my elementary and secondary education. As they continued to leave me out and experience more and more academic success, I began to see a different side of them. They didn't misbehave. Most attended church. Most received accolades from adults for being kind and trying hard in school. They were the Girls. I used to be one of them. Not anymore.

"We're not really friends anymore," said one of the Girls in fifth grade. Hoping that she was just having a bad day, I waited for the sting of her words to wear off. I thought she was my best friend. She knew all of my secret crushes. We celebrated multiple Halloweens at her church together. We spent hours playing Nancy Drew and Sims computer games—not to mention all of the days at the pool and sleepovers. I wasn't going to give up on this friendship. I insisted to myself that we would be best friends forever.

She wasn't just having a bad day, however. Over the next three years, I watched my relationships at school go from bad to worse. Looking back at it now, I think the primary reason for this shift wasn't meanness by the Girls, but the development of mature thoughts, feelings, and relationships during adolescence. Whereas young children can simply play together, without much need for deep communication, adolescents and adults crave friendships built on emotional intimacy. To develop emotional intimacy, friends must listen and selflessly care for one another. Listening to me requires more patience and time because my speech is slow and difficult to understand. The average adolescent and teenager is not patient enough to listen to most people, let alone me.

Further, the average adolescent is overly concerned about self-image—how will it look to be in public with a girl in a wheelchair who drools sometimes and talks "funny"? This is a hefty burden to expect adults to carry, let alone insecure teens. Finally, youth are simply trying to figure out their own lives and issues, having very little capacity to genuinely care about the deep issues of someone different than them.

How could I expect my childhood friendships to hold up under the weighted pressure of my ever-complex disability issues? What were they supposed to say when I first figured out that I wasn't going to attract the average guy? How were they supposed to respond when I expressed that I was sad that I couldn't do the same activities as them? I, too, wasn't mature enough to express my feelings about the disability-related complications of my life. It may have helped them know how to be my friend if I had the maturity to say, "I'm sorry it takes so much longer to have a conversation with me. Thanks for taking time to listen," or "I know it is too difficult to have me over to your house now that I'm bigger, so you should just invite yourself over to mine," or "I absolutely hate it when I laugh so hard that I drool and wet my pants."

Then again, maybe it would have made no difference at all. Maybe some people just aren't comfortable being close friends with someone with a disability. Maybe God, just as He equipped my family, equips certain jewels to be able to genuinely be friends with disabled individuals. In my case, my friends must be equipped in a way that helping me with everyday activities becomes second nature instead of a self-determined act of charity. Expecting elementary friends, bonded merely by a shared K-12 education, to be able to be genuine friends with me is a faulty expectation.

Faulty expectations would cause constant turmoil in my life and the lives of the Girls for the next seven years. Looking back, I can see the turmoil they must have been in. They didn't want to be my friends, but small-school etiquette and faith convictions made them feel guilty for not wanting to be my friend. In particular, two of the Girls would almost annually write me I'm-sorry-let's-be-friends letters. When Mom and I were cleaning out my childhood closet a few months ago, we found all of these letters. Mom's response was, "Oh, I didn't realize how many there were."

I did. Every time I would receive a letter written in colorful ink, my hopes would soar. "School will be better now. I'll have friends now." However, because the letters were written out of kindness-produced guilt, the sentiments never led to genuine friendship. The Girls may have sat with me at lunch for a while, but the invitations to all but one party would never come. One of the Girls may have volunteered to be my locker partner, but there would be no genuine bonding before or after school. I may have been invited to join the Girls for junior prom, after never being invited to join any homecoming group, but I would still not be invited to get ready or ride with them.

The letters almost made life in the small-town school worse because I had no consistency or peace. I wasn't mature enough to put up boundaries to safeguard my emotions and walk away from my tumultuous relationship with the Girls, which never left anyone happy. When some of the Girls started sitting with me at lunch, the other Girls weren't happy with the new arrangement. They made this apparent to the whole cafeteria by sitting at the table across the room from my table. Even if I had wanted to switch tables, I wouldn't have been able to sit at that table because it was surrounded by a wall, lockers, and other tables. My wheelchair wouldn't have made it through. My heart goes out to the Girls who felt compelled to sit by me but had to face this harsh verdict from their fellow Girls. To appease everyone, the compelled Girls would rotate between the two tables. Most notably, this situation allowed the compelled Girls to maintain their reputations of being kind and sweet.

 I internalized the humiliation that this caused me every day. The current, more confident Janae would have released them from their compulsory kindness and gained the peace of mind that comes with setting boundaries necessary to protect my emotions. The teenage Janae was torn in many different directions. Just as my emotions went toward the humiliation direction, I remembered that I was being fed by a middle-aged woman. What high schoolers in their right mind would be thrilled to sit at a lunch table with a disabled student and adult para? Further, I remembered my coughing fits that caused food to occasionally fly out of my mouth at random times due to my uncoordinated tongue and throat muscles. Thankfully, I usually had the most appropriate aim possible, but sometimes spontaneity got in the way. Combining these disability-related annoyances, I felt I should be thankful that anyone would sit by me. Had I known the plethora of genuine friends my future held, I would have happily opted to sit alone.

During my senior year, much to the Girls' awkward chagrin, I found out about a Halloween party. Note that the Girls usually seemed to keep their parties quiet from me. I'm thankful for their discreetness because, even if I knew that I was generally uninvited to parties, I was blissfully ignorant of the details. I wasn't so fortunate on Halloween of my senior year. Still having an immature and illogical desire to be one of the Girls, when I found out about the Halloween party, I got myself a pity invite. Why? Why did I do that? After Mom dropped me off at the party, I gingerly made my way inside the walk-out basement. I hadn't been in this Girl's house since elementary. As usual, people were polite, but not overly friendly to me. There was food that no one fed me and drinks that no one gave me. This wasn't surprising enough to upset me. The upsetting surprise was what came next.

> [Janae Hofer] is doing something 4 Halloween yay!
> —October 30, 2008

> [Janae Hofer] hates school!
> —November 3, 2008

Although the hosting Girl had warned me that there would be outdoor games as a way to dissuade me from coming to the party, I imagined that my involvement in the games would be similar to involvement in outdoor games at youth group. My imagination was completely naive. Why I thought the Girls would all of the sudden begin treating me with the loving inclusiveness that I experienced at my youth group in Omaha is beyond me.

When it was time for the outdoor games, it was dark. I was informed that I could either sit outside in the dark or wait inside. However, the basement lights also needed to be off because they wanted complete darkness for their game. As people began moving outside, I opted to stay inside where at least I would be warm. They shut the door and turned off the lights. I sat there in dark silence.

At first, I thought someone would come back to check on me in a few minutes. At youth group, whenever the group did an activity that I couldn't do, they figured out a way to have me cheer from the sidelines. My genuine friends waved and shouted at me from time to time, if not taking turns sitting out with me. I was never left alone. But, here I was, in a dark basement all alone.

As the minutes passed, I felt more and more trapped and

depressed. I started tearing up, thinking of all the people I wanted to be with. I wanted to be with my family, who were eating dinner at my grandma's with my out-of-town aunt and uncle. I wanted some of my genuine youth group friends to fling open the door and rescue me from this darkness. I wanted to be anywhere but here.

"God, help me get out of here soon. Why did I tell Mom not to pick me up until 10:00 p.m.—it's only 7:30 p.m.?" I didn't have a cell phone until college because we hadn't figured out how to adapt one to make it usable yet. I couldn't call Mom. I couldn't call anyone. All I could do was sit and pace in the darkness as I prayed and hoped that college would bring a better life.

> [Janae Hofer] finally got a cell phone!
> —June 3, 2009

By the time people began coming back inside, I was in no state to be at a party. Definitely not a party with people who left me in the dark for at least an hour, if not longer. I asked one of the nice, quiet non-Girls to help me call Mom to pick me up. As I left the party noticeably early, the hosting Girl looked surprised for a moment before saying, "I warned you that we would be playing outside. What did you expect?"

I had no response, as I was simply trying to hold back tears until I got into the car.

≈

Looking back, I'm disgusted that I allowed myself to get sucked into the Halloween party after I'd finally had enough courage to establish healthy boundaries for junior prom. For the first time ever, the Girls invited me to join them at a school dance. I was thrilled. As you already know, Mom spared no expense, buying me the pink prom dress of my dreams and scheduling appointments for me to get my hair and makeup done.

[Janae Hofer] is worried about prom.
—March 4, 2008

However, not long after the verbal invitation came the complications. First, because I couldn't get into any of their houses, I was expected to get ready on my own. My church friends would have lifted me in my manual wheelchair into any house—they still do. Second, no one wanted to ride in my van with Mom driving. My parents offered to let one of the licensed Girls drive, but none of them were comfortable with that. Then, my parents offered to pay for the majority of a limo so that I could ride with them, and then Mom would follow behind with my electric wheelchair. The group was too big to fit in one limo, and the Girls were unwilling to split up. Even though they would have to take multiple cars anyway, they felt it was for unfair some of them to ride in a limo and others not to. They weren't happy with the idea of having people rotate riding, and they couldn't afford to get a second limo. Thankfully my parents were wise enough not to offer to pay for a second limo. So as we approached prom, I was to get ready on my own and drive to the restaurant and prom with Mom. The final straw was when I realized there would be no one to feed me at the restaurant. Things looked grim and unbearably lonely.

I called Heather. I was crying on the phone, telling her all of the complications. Defensively, she suggested that she, Marietta, Kristin, and Katie celebrate prom with me instead. After I immaturely announced my new prom dates on Facebook, one of the Girls angrily said, "I worked so hard to include you!" I wish I would have had the courage to inform the Girls of my new plans in person, but I was barely confident enough to even break out on my own, let alone explain why to their face and undergo their all-too-common gaslighting. Given their gaslighting tendencies, the reaction would have likely been the same whether they read my change of plans on Facebook or received the word in person.

Not going to prom with them turned out to be one of my best decisions as a teenager because I finally learned how to identify real friends. My church friends made the thirty-minute drive to my house to get ready with me. They all found formal dresses even though it wasn't their prom. We danced and laughed in the bathroom, taking funny photos until my adoring father put the corsage on my wrist. My parents and I had to be on time for prom because Jamison (my older brother) was being crowned prom king. His coronation was the only reason I made an appearance at my actual prom.

After his coronation and a few quick photos with him and a few nice upperclassmen, I met my friends at Cheesecake Factory. We deemed the night "antiprom" and formed the Sisterhood of Cheesecake. Katie fed me. Heather helped me in the bathroom. I'm sure that Kristin was instrumental in paving the way through the crowded restaurant. And, Marietta made sure that my face was clean between our laughing spells. I think they made a special point of fighting over who "got to" feed me. Antiprom was repeated my senior year. The Sisterhood of Cheesecake lives on today.

> [Janae Hofer] is gonna go 2 prom 4 20 min then going out w/ her BFFs 2 Cheesecake Factory, then post-prom!
> —March 21, 2008

Now it's time to shine the light on my genuine friends, made of the finest material—gems and precious metals refined through their own trials of life and proven true. You have already met Heather—my first genuine friend. I count myself extremely blessed that we became friends in junior high. In reality, Heather didn't leave me much choice. She is not who I would have picked to be my childhood best friend. Our fashion couldn't clash more. We have different movie and music tastes. Our decorating styles clash so much that when Mom suggested that we be roommates, I shuddered at the thought. To give a visual, imagine Heather's large SPAM flag hanging above my pink orchid. Not exactly how you would picture two peas in a pod. Thankfully, we at least enjoy the same food so we can eat together. Still, our unified faith and steadfast love for each other bonds us even more.

I met my unlikely friend in fifth grade when my family began attending my childhood church. God must have planned that my family would switch to this church the year that my placeholder friends would start slipping away. If I had had my way, we would have attended a church in the small town where I attended school. However, my parents found no theologically sound church in town. Thus, they elected to make the twenty-minute drive into Omaha each Sunday. Omaha is a larger city where my dad ran his businesses, and we did all of our shopping. Because we lived in the country in between Omaha and Fort Calhoun, but only attended school in Fort Calhoun, I often simply tell inquiring individuals that I'm from Omaha. This might also be residue from my less-than-fond memories of my school.

The first thing I noticed about Heather was her outdatedly large hairbow. It took Heather a while to convince me that we could be friends, but her persistent kindness won me over. I don't think she was trying to convince me to be friends as much as she was just being her caring self. She has always been confident enough that she didn't need anyone to be her friend who didn't want to be. The characteristic that drew me to Heather was the way she treated me like everyone else. Not only did she talk to me like I didn't have cerebral palsy, but she was patient to listen. Her patient listening allowed me to converse with her like I didn't have cerebral palsy. I took full advantage of the opportunity to talk her ear off whenever I got the chance. Even in my family, being able to talk as much as I wanted didn't necessarily mean I was heard. Heather is the first person who ever made a point of hearing every word I said. She was only in sixth grade when I noticed this trait.

Once I realized that Heather listened, I was desperate to be best friends. Still, I was overwhelmingly worried she would turn her back on me like the Girls. I wanted to make sure we had common interests. I tried overly hard to like her music and be excited about her movies. Once she caught on that I was showing interest just to be her friend, she slowly convinced me that she just liked me for me.

Today, we're both confident in our friendship and our own interests. She loves me even with my trendy shoes and affinity for romantic comedies. I love her with her individual style and appreciation for less-cliché-girl movies.

Heather is also special because she's the first friend who took care of me. I was too self-conscious to let her feed me for years. Even before that, allowing her to hold my drink while I slurped through a straw also made me nervous. I was much more insecure than she was, so I worried that she wouldn't want to be friends after helping me with disability-related tasks. I don't remember how old I was when she first fed me, but she most likely fed me a piece of pizza or chips during youth group. My parents were our junior high youth group leaders, so the feeding transition from Mom to Heather likely occurred in ninth grade. I never remember not being able to eat at a youth group event, and my parents no longer helped with my youth group when I was in high school. With as much thought as I put into having Heather feed me, she has made it clear that she put almost no thought into the implications on our friendship. Helping me has been a natural part of life for her. Whether getting me in and out of cars and houses, or putting on my shoes and coat, she has never failed to be up for the challenge—rarely ever being uncomfortable.

Heather's assistance gave me confidence that I could find other friends who would be comfortable feeding me, driving my vehicle, and helping me in the restroom. This assistance is necessary for natural friendships. How am I to go to dinner with someone who is uncomfortable with feeding me? Sure, I can bring a caregiver, but at a certain point, if I'm going to be close friends with someone, they have to be comfortable with helping me with daily living activities.

My friendship with Heather was the gateway to my other friendships in youth group. I was more confident when I was with Heather, so I made other lifelong friends more easily because I was able to be myself. You've already met them in the prom story. Although I only saw my youth group friends once or twice a week, these times gave me enough joy to propel me through the hard times at school.

I became so close to these friends that I feared that I wouldn't push myself to make new friends in college. As a result, when I moved to Grace University, I decided it was best for me to attend Sunday services at a church with girls from my dorm hall. Still, my high school experience had left scars that caused me to doubt whether I would even make friends in college. I was happy that I had my own dorm room with a connected bathroom so that I would be able to hide from the mean girls that I anticipated would be in college the same as in high school. I comforted myself at the prospect of moving away from home by telling myself that, if nothing else, I could get a takeout box from the cafeteria so that I wouldn't have to eat at a table alone. Heather agreed to be my caregiver for a couple of nights each week, so I was overjoyed that I would at least see someone who cared about me throughout the week. I also told myself that at least I would have Sunday lunches with my family. I was fully prepared to embrace the loneliness of dorm life.

I couldn't have been more wrong. After the first few nights of going to bed by 10:00 p.m., I don't know if I ever went to bed by 10:00 p.m. for the rest of college. I quickly realized that people were eager to hang out with me, genuinely enjoying my company. I was surprised at how quickly the students recognized my intelligence and humor. I even had guy friends, which was almost an entirely new concept to me. Moreover, because the girls lived with me day in and day out, they easily became comfortable helping me eat and use the bathroom. I formed so many lifelong friendships during undergrad.

I believe my vast number of friends is actually a large part thanks to my rough high school experience. My unpleasant experience gave me a unique perspective going into college. Even though I doubted whether I would make friends, I knew that it would be up to me to initiate friendships and make people feel comfortable around me.

One way I did this was to put a short explanation of my cerebral palsy outside of my dorm room so that people could read it at their leisure and better understand how to interact with me. Also, whenever I got the sense that someone was nervous about interacting with me, I said little comments to put them at ease, "Don't worry if you don't understand everything I say, you will get better over time."

Hard work on my part, and selflessness on the part of girls in my dorm, yielded many lifelong friends. A few of these friends are friends that I know I could call at any moment and they would come to my aide. Other friends are simply friends who I could easily call to catch up over dinner and coffee, and who I know would have no problem helping me eat or use the restroom. Both types of friends spur me on even today. I believe that the relationships I made at Grace University will stand the test of time and prove to be some of the most rewarding relationships of my life.

Following my years at Grace, making deep friendships shifted back to being more difficult. When I don't have the opportunity to live day in and day out with girls, I believe it is more difficult to establish that level of comfort with each other. Questions of "Who feeds her when we go out?" never seem to naturally resolve themselves. However, because I already have a solid base of friends, the lack of new postcollege friendships doesn't bother me much. How could I possibly pour into more friends' lives with my limited energy and time? I have virtually all of the support I could ever hope for from my preexisting friends. They not only know how to care for me physically, but also emotionally and spiritually.

This is not to say that I haven't developed any extremely close friendships after graduating from Grace. Most close friendships have developed through employer-employee relationships with my most trusted caregivers. Not all caregivers I've hired fall into this category. Some couldn't be trusted, causing me to worry about the theft of my belongings and financial information. Other caregivers are simply "good enough" for the time being, but not proactive with meeting my needs.

Yet I can identify the caregivers who truly care about me as a beloved friend because they not only go above and beyond to meet my needs, but also remain in my employment for years on end even when their life transitions into new phases. These types of friends are one of the most abundant graces in my life because they provide constant physical and emotional support for me. I feel safe and not alone when they care for me. I know they'll do what needs to be done even if I'm too weak from physical or emotional pain to direct them. Whereas my other close friends can only be physically present with me sometimes, these friends are consistent with me. These friends are my favorite part of having cerebral palsy. How many adults have an excuse to see their friends on a daily basis?

To be clear, my caregivers who become my friends hang out with me both on and off the clock. Although some might think differentiating between paid hours and friend hours may be difficult, we manage quite well thanks to open communication and selflessness on both our parts. For example, if I'm going out with a friend who is also a caregiver, I'll make sure the nighttime routine is as quick as possible when we get home. I do this by setting out my medication and pajamas ahead of time. I also tell them to set my clothes on my dresser instead of putting them away when they change me into my pajamas. These small differentiations wouldn't work with every caregiver friend, but not every caregiver is a close friend. This is the same way I treat friends who aren't caregivers. My friends love helping me, but I try to make it as easy as possible on them as to not make them feel taken advantage of. In addition to a more minimal bedtime routine, I also try to reduce the amount of help I need by simply asking my friends to put dirty dishes in the sink instead of washing them. I can have a paid caregiver wash them the next morning. At times I feel that these habits are more for my peace of mind than for my friends, as they frequently insist on hanging up clothes and doing the dishes anyway.

Although the path to finding true friends was difficult, I'm so thankful that God, in His grace, allowed me to find these gems. Stories of them in this chapter and other chapters should prove that I have priceless gems for friends as opposed to the placeholder jewelry that many people experience in friendship. Having friends that I'm unwaveringly confident in is the biggest blessing of cerebral palsy—without a doubt, hands down. My friends truly help me be grateful for my disability because I never question whether they are authentic. People who care for your most basic physical needs will undoubtedly be there to weather almost any storm of life. Although I may struggle with disability-induced depression on a number of days, the depression fades during moments with my friends. These truly are moments woven together with the golden thread of God's grace.

The Single Life

When people see a severely disabled woman going about her business in a wheelchair, their first thought is not about whether she's single. This is likely true no matter how well dressed the woman is. Even if her hair and makeup are perfect, the first thought is related to the wheelchair. *Why is she in a wheelchair? She has such a pretty smile for being so severely disabled.* The thought process is not *Why is she here alone?* or *She has such a pretty smile; I want her number.*

My inability to attract men's attention, in general, has been one of the most difficult aspects of my disability to emotionally overcome. I know it's shocking that a girl who couldn't feed herself didn't get asked to prom. I mean, come on, didn't the high school guys know that I couldn't dance either? Didn't they appreciate the natural physical boundaries that my wheelchair provided? Every high school guy should have been clamoring at my feet. Not!

Although I had crushes in high school, my heart was never broken, and the lack of attention never bothered me in an overwhelming way. This cool-headed attitude was because I had a plan. I was going to follow in my parents' footsteps and avoid dating in high school only to go to Christian university and meet the love of my life in the first semester of my freshman year.

Ready?

Go!

God didn't get the memo. Actually, He definitely got the memo. He just didn't implement the memo. Although I had more guy friends in college and fell in love for the first and only time thus far in my life, I graduated from Grace University without my MRS sealed with a diamond ring. "That's okay, God. An attorney wouldn't pair well with a pastor anyway. New plan—I'll get married after I become an attorney."

Ready?

Go!

Four years later. Still single. Practicing attorney. "Okay, God, we talked about this. It is time to bring me a husband. I know I'm not perfect, but lots of less perfect people get married."

After realizing that the Christian community at large had accepted online dating, I decided to try it. Just hit a few keys and find the love of your life, right? Not for me. Many first dates and wasted hours later, I switched off online dating.

Twenty-eight. I'm single at twenty-eight. Twenty-eight is almost thirty. I'm not going to be married by thirty! Why?

For years, I blamed my cerebral palsy for every failed relationship and my perpetual singleness. However, somewhere along the way, my mindset switched from hating singleness all the time with brief moments of contentment to enjoying singleness most of the time with brief moments of discontentment. This enjoyment isn't due to a lack of desire to marry. I still desire to find a truer version of the love that I first experienced in college.

~ Moments of Grace ~

However, as I truly believe that God is loving and good, I'm more convinced that He isn't holding out on me.

I finally found a church family who truly loves and cares for me. From the age of twenty-one to twenty-five, I absolutely hated going to church. One primary reason for this was that every Sunday I was nauseated by the scene of picture-perfect young dating, engaged, and married couples. I went to a large hip church, so the percentage of young couples far exceeded the percentage of seasoned families and older individuals. It was disheartening to look around the room and see that seemingly everyone had someone but me. The Christmas Eve service was the worst.

But when I found the right church for me, my weekly hatred of singleness eventually faded. The church is filled with single women, widows and widowers, elderly couples, families, and a proportional number of young couples. Now, instead of dreading church, I look forward to this weekly fellowship where I feel the most complete and at peace. So much so that I wonder how my church family would even react if "the one" suddenly became two. Right now, when I walk in the door, I'm greeted with kisses and conversations from older women who genuinely care about me. The older men smile and nod at me with thankfulness in their eyes that I'm a member. I find comfort sitting next to my fellow single friend and dog mom, Amy, feeling complete as I worship with my church family. Amy is a more seasoned single woman who has shown me how to be a godly, professional single woman without becoming bitter and giving up on the idea of marriage.

Yes, at my church I feel so complete that, this year, I told Mom that if my parents wanted to go to their own church's Christmas Eve service, I would be fine with them just dropping me off at my church. I smile as I say this because, not too many years ago, the thought of attending a Christmas Eve service alone would have been the most sobering image to me, right next to scrooge alone in his house. But I'm never alone at my church. I'm with family—a family that I have chosen to love and who has chosen to love me, just me—single or not.

For some reason, it is best for me to be single now, so I'll enjoy my freedom. I'll enjoy sleeping when I want and taking up the whole bed along with the entirety of the closet and master bathroom. I'll enjoy being able to tithe to any organization I want for any amount I see fit. I'll enjoy being able to fill my house with the decorations I love and having my girls over any time. Finally, I'll enjoy spending all the time I want with my side of the family.

When I focus on the blessings of being single, it's far easier for me to avoid acting out of desperation. At one point in my life, I was so desperate for any attention from any guy that I allowed myself to be treated as less than a treasured daughter of the King. Instead of behaving like a princess, I behaved as a starving dog, jumping at any scraps a guy would throw to the ground and allowing myself to be kicked.

Now that I see myself through God's eyes, I see that my disability actually protects me from marrying a selfish man. If I ever do marry, although we'll have difficult discussions about my cerebral palsy, his actions and words will demonstrate that he sees me through God's eyes and loves me as Christ. Although I have yet to meet a man who sees and loves me in that way, I know it's possible because my friends see me through the eyes of God.

What does God see in this decrepit, wheelchair-bound body? He sees beauty in the way He made me. He sees hands worn from persevering, hard work. He sees a woman who has risen to the challenge of doing her best to provide for herself and manage a home. He sees a woman who laughs with joy. He sees a woman who is up for any adventure, whether being carted up a mountain or winched up a windmill. He sees a woman who has so much more to offer others than even she realizes. He sees an imperfect woman who loves Him. He sees me. And that's what my future husband will have to see. Unless I meet a man who undoubtedly realizes that what he sees far outweighs any disability-related negatives in the same ways as my friends and family, I choose to live my life content in my pursuit of God, the only perfect companion.

Part Three

EDUCATIONAL ENDEAVORS

Beginning

By God's grace, the lack of oxygen at birth didn't hinder my intellectual abilities. Somehow Mom was confident in this from day one. As the severity of my physical limitations became more apparent, she held fast to the idea that even if I couldn't find a job, I'd just keep going to school and acquiring more and more doctorates. This resolve on her part is extraordinary to me. She didn't grow up in a family that focused on higher education. As you already know, her family life was centered on farming. The fact that she was forward-thinking enough to think outside the box when I was as young as two shows how much she loves me.

Despite Mom's resolute attitude toward my education and intellect, navigating the educational system would ultimately push me to my breaking point. By strength that can only be attributed to God, I graduated from Creighton School of Law ranked 15 out of 122.

The Young Lawyer

Before law school, however, there was preschool. Although my parents elected not to send my older brother to preschool, they felt it was best for me to attend so that I could receive physical, occupational, and speech therapy. Even though I'd been receiving therapy from the time I was a baby, preschool was the natural avenue for continuing these services. I don't have many memories of preschool.

One memory is my logical argument with the other children on why Santa Claus didn't exist. Looking back now, this was probably the first indicator that I would be a decent attorney. I might be biased, but the fact that a three-year-old pointed to the impossibility of Santa Claus delivering gifts everywhere in one night seems fairly advanced. Further, I questioned how he got into houses with no fireplaces; how his sleigh could be big enough to hold every present, but small enough to land on a roof; and how he could possibly know where everyone lived. Naturally, my teachers tried to silence my critiques of this vital childhood myth. Unfortunately for them, my parents took the approach of never lying to their children, not even about something as harmless as Santa Claus.

The Small-Town School

Following preschool, I entered kindergarten at the small-town school that I previously mentioned. I remember enjoying school, but I hated being pulled out of class for therapy. Given my parents' high concerns about my academic development, they had to find a balance between working on the physical aspects of my development at the expense of missing class. For example, if I was to work on walking with my walker, I might miss a reading lesson.

Wisely, my parents attempted to direct my education in a way that as the years went on, academics became more and more the focus. Another avenue of therapy that kept my academics at the focal point of my education was outpatient therapy after school. Not only were my therapists at this center top-notch, but I was able to receive services without missing class.

Not everyone understood or agreed with my parents' academic-centered approach to my education. However, Mom summarized the reasoning the best: "She'll never walk on her own no matter how much therapy, but she might be able to pursue a career with the right academics." I'll be forever grateful that they took this approach. Not only did my parents' approach open career doors, but also, it normalized my life in a way that gave me more in common with my peers. Instead of worrying about getting to the next level in physical therapy, I was worried about tomorrow's science test along with my classmates.

Broken for the First Time

Before I even turned eight, I faced my first severe educational challenge at the hands of someone who was supposed to ensure my safety. From kindergarten to my senior year of high school, I had an individual paraprofessional with me at school. The majority of my paras were everything that one could hope for in a para for a young child—kind, dedicated, and eager to help me excel. However, I wasn't always so fortunate. Early in my education, I had a borderline abusive para. She didn't agree with my parents' philosophy of academics over physical development.

Her emphasis on the physical was so severe that it was dangerous. Instead of helping me pull down my pants and pivot to the toilet, she made me pull down my own pants, allowing me to fall to the floor and refusing to help me up. I struggled to get up as she scolded me for not trying harder. If I told her that Mom helped me wipe at home, she said that she would take me away from my parents if that was true because they were hindering my development. Thus, I had to wipe myself and figure out a way to put soap on my hands to wash them. Even worse was eating with her. Frequently, and especially when other adults weren't watching, this para refused to feed me. I either ate by face-planting into my food or trying to pick up my food and shove it into my mouth. The problem with picking up my food was that my hand muscles would grasp it too tight, causing the food to crumble. This also often resulted in my clothing being covered in food.

To cope with this situation, I prayed that she would be sick every day, which meant I would have a nicer fill-in aid help me. One time she injured herself, which caused her to miss a week or two of work. I'm ashamed to admit that I praised God for this brief reprieve. Another coping mechanism was that I begged Mom to let me bring the negligent para candy every day, hoping that the candy might cause her to be nicer to me.

As with most abusive situations, the problem got progressively worse over time. Although Mom wasn't able to detect the problem in the beginning, and I, as a young child, wasn't able to adequately grasp or understand what was happening, Mom eventually caught on. Thankfully, my teacher became increasingly concerned about my academic performance. As you can imagine, if my para wouldn't even help me use the bathroom, she was virtually no help in the classroom either. I was focusing so hard on physically completing classwork that I couldn't learn the material. Sometimes she tried to have me write the numbers for my math assignment with a pencil, refusing to allow me to dictate the answer to her. To date, I have never clearly written one letter or number with the hands God gave me. When she was satisfied that I'd tried hard enough to write with a pencil, she then made me type the number on my keyboard. By this time, the class was already moving on to the next activity.

I felt hopeless and unintelligent. Seeing my struggles snapped my teacher into action. She and my already-concerned mother kept a detailed journal of the everyday incidents, which eventually amounted to enough leverage to secure her resignation. Of course, if Mom would had known the danger that I was in every time I went to the bathroom, my parents would have removed me from the situation immediately. Still, despite my inability to effectively communicate, God gave others discernment enough to rescue me from the situation.

Rebuilding

My most influential para helped me from fourth grade through my senior year in high school. I would have loved to have her help me in college, but she was wise enough to see that, even if she could, having a sixty-year-old woman hanging around with me would severely limit my normal college experience. Her name is Mrs. Schuler. When she started, I imagine that I was quite similar to a broken-winged baby bird. I lacked any confidence in my abilities. She helped me succeed at my academics, while still encouraging me to learn how to type on my own. I imagine that it was difficult for her to know when to make me type and when to let me dictate. To be sure, my answers were significantly better when I dictated them. I got frustrated with my slow typing speed and wrote short, insufficient answers. Yet she saw that it was important to develop my typing and computer skills as much as possible before entering the real world. Although my high school GPA might have been higher if she had let me dictate all of the time, I believe that she found the appropriate balance, considering that I ended up as an attorney.

Along with encouraging me to do my best in school, she was undoubtedly 100 percent on my team. When I was in junior high, I had a speech therapist at school who couldn't understand me at all. On one particular day, this therapist told me to say the word *symptom*. When I said *symptom*, she immediately became appalled that I'd told her to "sit down." When she reported my unruly behavior to Mrs. Schuler, Mrs. Schuler listened to me enough to get to the bottom of this uncharacteristically defiant behavior. I don't believe I ever met with that particular speech therapist again.

Yet Mrs. Schuler still had to be patient and wise enough to determine when I was actually being mischievous. I often turned off my keyboard and told her that it wasn't working so that she would allow me to dictate. She caught on most of the time. Also, in sixth grade, I was very insecure about Spanish lessons, so I tried to hide in the bathroom the whole time. This, too, she picked up on. She was patient enough to find humor in my little stunts. For example, in fifth grade, the whole class was required to stay in from recess and write our names fifty times. I realized that if I typed my name once, I could copy and paste it five times, copy and paste the set of five, and finally copy and paste the set of ten four more times. The end result was "Janae Hofer" typed fifty times in under five minutes. Mrs. Schuler congratulated me for my efficient, creative ingenuity, but only let me get away with it once.

She also became my best friend at school from seventh grade until I graduated. The only reason I enjoyed going to school was because I would get to talk to her all day. She taught me so much not only about life, but also about thinking and relating to people with different beliefs. We didn't agree on religion or politics, but given that I was an unashamedly opinionated kid when she started, we debated these topics. Obviously, our debates became more sophisticated from George W. Bush's first election when I was in fourth grade to Barack Obama's first election when I was a senior. My parents weren't overly concerned with my exposure to these beliefs because Mrs. Schuler's genuine aim was to develop my critical thinking, not to merely sway me to her side. I attribute my balanced, well-reasoned political views to her even though she likely wouldn't agree with most of my current beliefs.

Every moment with her was a moment of grace. She taught me to be confident in who I am. I never wanted to be associated with special education out of fear of perpetuating the idea that my intelligence wasn't as high as the average. She said, "Whether you like it or not, you are special ed, but being in special ed doesn't mean you're dumb." When I worried about having to do things differently, she patiently told me to get over it and be who I am. Yet when I didn't make it into the advanced math classes, she consoled me that I would still do great things.

Mind you, that the people in the advanced math classes were seen as the Academic Superstars of the school, leaving others feeling doomed to a life of subpar performance. She wouldn't let me settle for subpar performance. I was thankful that she didn't give up on me when I finally achieved all As my senior year of high school, and the top grade in my college English class where I wrote my first legal paper. I would go on to continue to get all As throughout my entire undergraduate career.

The Teacher

Mrs. Schuler wasn't the only educator that invested in me during my secondary years. Mrs. Becker was my junior high English teacher, ninth grade speech teacher, and coach. Known for having high expectations, she was also the most invested teacher I have ever met. She wouldn't only plan a week-long Shakespeare camp each school year, complete with student-created sets and movies, but she also came up with fun writing units, such as "Write Your Own Mystery" and book-themed dress-up days. Under her instruction, I created a family tree that my grandma still has to this day.

More importantly, I developed my love for writing. She encouraged and challenged me to be a better writer even though she made it clear that I was already talented beyond my age. She wasn't easy on me though. One time, I was upset that I was overlooked by the Academic Superstars in a book discussion group. Mrs. Becker gently said, "Well, if you read the book more thoroughly than them, it will be harder for them to overlook your input." I think what she was getting at was, "Yes, Janae, people will always overlook you, so, like it or not, you will have to work harder and be better." I hope she's proud of how I implemented her words of wisdom throughout my life.

Beyond junior high English, Mrs. Becker was also my high school speech teacher. Again, she encouraged me to fine-tune my research and succinct writing skills. She encouraged me to develop my speaking skills despite my speech impediment. Though she didn't know that I would end up as an attorney, she undoubtedly knew that these skills would be critical for the rest of my life. I was robbed of my chance to take junior year literature with her, as she was unsurprisingly snatched up by a private school. However, before she left, she also gave me the opportunity to be the cheerleading manager. She let me keep track of points and schedules for the cheerleaders, along with assisting at tryouts. By this time, she knew how desperately I was trying to fit in. As far as it depended on her, she wanted to help make me feel like I belonged. I never felt like I belonged with the cheerleaders, but I felt like I belonged with her. To this day, we're still friends.

∻ *Janae Hofer* ∾

Trapped in Comparison

My inner conflict with the Academic Superstars should be obvious by now. The conflict began in third grade when I understandably wasn't selected to be a member of High Ability Learners (HAL). HAL was the group in my elementary school that catered to the Academic Superstars. When I still had the borderline abusive para in third grade, being in HAL was so beyond my reach. Perhaps this was the first psychological effect of my cerebral palsy—I knew I was smart, but I couldn't show my intelligence. Therefore, I questioned whether I was actually intelligent. Instead of defining myself by what God had given me in terms of talents, I defined myself by what others could see. This trend would continue until I was twenty-six years old. But the root was that seemingly innocent HAL group.

When Mrs. Schuler came along, I achieved enough academic success to be in HAL about half the time. This gave me more confidence, but I still experienced inner turmoil. I'm a perfectionist, so I wanted to get perfect grades. I couldn't achieve this until my senior year, so my attitude constantly fluctuated between trying so hard that I was overwhelmed and not trying at all. This isn't uncommon, but imagine knowing that you could write an A-quality essay in a tenth of the time if you could only dictate instead of finger poking it on a special keyboard with holes drilled in a hard plastic overlay to guide my fingers to the correct keys. My frustration became even more severe when the Academic Superstars received continual accolades. I, on the other hand, was just under the cut. More frustrating still was that I saw the Academic Superstars comparing homework, refining their answers until they were perfect. They had each other's backs. You know by now that none of my classmates had my back. I had no one to refine my answers. My Bs were self-earned, but they weren't good enough to put me in the top half of my high school class.

As if I wasn't already frustrated enough with my academic performance, my high school guidance counselor matter-of-factly informed my entire class that in order to get accepted into a four-year university, we needed to be in the top half of the class. I often wonder if she neglected to notice that people at the bottom half of the class still had a 3.2 GPA. When I informed my parents that I would be going to community college, they subtly redirected my focus to four-year institutions.

In fact, my senior year, when I informed Dad that I was going to be a paralegal, he said, "Well, you might as well try to be an attorney because you will be that much more qualified for any job you want." I shudder to think where I would be if I didn't have parents who believed in me, not only in word but in deed and money. When I got accepted to Grace University, I received scholarships for almost half of my tuition. Surprisingly, one scholarship was the result of a recommendation by the same guidance counselor who had originally dashed my hopes of attending a university.

Even with these scholarships, the financial burden associated with me attending college was vastly more than the average. My parents demonstrated their unwavering faith in me by not only paying to renovate a dorm to make it handicapped accessible, but also by paying thousands of dollars for caregivers and scribes to assist me during college. They did this even as they were on the verge of bankruptcy during the long recession that hit the real estate market. Government aid was available to cover part of the cost of caregivers and scribes, but the process that my caregivers and scribes had to go through to get paid took so long that, had it not been for my parents, I doubt I could have kept employees. Without these employees, I couldn't have succeeded in college.

I would be lying if I denied that I was never motivated out of anger over how I was perceived in high school. By nature,

I'm a perfectionist. Among other drawbacks of perfectionism is the desire to prove that I'm worthwhile. I didn't feel worthwhile in high school because I compared my performance to that of the Academic Superstars, continually coming up short. This comparison caused anger to build and, at times, fuel my achievements. Slowly, as I learn the pitfalls of comparison, God has taught me to find my identity in Him alone, not in how others perceive me. When I find my identity in God, who always sees me as worthy, I can set aside my insecure anger and motives. By His grace, I continue to strive to be motivated by my desire to please and glorify Him instead of my anger about being misperceived by others.

> [Janae Hofer] moves out tomorrow! Goodbye, Fort Calhoun, I won't miss you! I will, however, miss Hidden Acres, which includes my home, my family, my pets, and my neighbors (aka my grandparents) ... but I'm excited!
> —August 14, 2009

> Today I'm feeling old because my ten-year high school reunion is tomorrow. I'll not be attending because, although I wasn't bullied, high school holds no fond memories for me that I wish to reminisce about. No one owes me an apology, but there's no denying the fact that I just didn't fit, which resulted in four years of insecurity and dreading school. Why go back to a place that holds nothing but memories of anxiety and never measuring up?
> Still, I think we need to reject the notion that everyone should love high school, and if they don't, someone is always to blame. I wouldn't trade my high school experience for one of bliss. Although not true at the time, I'm thankful for my high school career

because it prepared me for the real world. Unlike church and Bible college, where I truly felt like I belonged, high school made me tough and prepared me for real life where 95 percent of people are polite to the disabled girl, but I'll never be on the inner circle. As in high school, my intelligence will routinely be overlooked. The difference between now and ten years ago is that I don't let myself become insecure. I don't bend over backward trying to fit in, getting dismayed when I don't. I don't get upset when sometimes people are nice to me simply so they can pat themselves on the back for being nice to the girl in a wheelchair. High school taught me how to have realistic expectations for life, along with how to cling to God and the truth that I'm loved by Him and others when I feel utterly alone in a crowded room. It taught me the value and qualities of good friends. It caused me to grow infinitely closer to my sweet mother, whose loving face was waiting for me at the end of each awkward day. For these blessings, I'm grateful.

—May 10, 2019

Days of Grace (University)

Saying that my years at Grace University were the best years of my life thus far is not an overstatement by any means. A quiet, unpopular, average student became an outgoing, popular, excellent student in a matter of weeks. I was nervous to move to the dorms, but obviously, I was more excited because I had a corner of my room dedicated to college packing beginning in May.

Choosing to attend Grace University was one of the best decisions of my life. Once I received the acceptance letter, the Dean of Women set out to make me feel welcome and at home.

She served as one of my most significant mentors from then until she passed away from cancer during my second year of law school. I made it through the service without crying, but then was bawling too hard to attend the reception luncheon in any dignified manner.

In addition to the Dean of Women, having my uncle as a professor in college made me feel more comfortable right away. Although he didn't understand why I would want to spend my last precollege summer doing homework, he granted my request for the syllabus for a class that I would be taking with him in the fall. This gave me confidence by allowing me to get ahead and remove some of the stress in the fall.

When I entered college, receiving good enough grades to be admitted to law school wasn't a foregone conclusion. I was merely trying to perform the best I could and trust God with the outcome. To my astonishment, academics were tremendously easier for me when I had scribes to type all of my homework and exams—I never typed one assignment or exam because the scribes decreased the time by tenfold. My peers were astonished that I was weeks ahead in every syllabus. I thought, *Why wouldn't I be? This is so much better than getting homework assigned the day before it is due like in high school.* I also had to plan to work ahead in the event that a scribe unexpectedly couldn't work the day before an assignment was due. How stressful it would have been to have a lifestyle of completing assignments hours before they were due, just hoping that nothing messed up the scribe's schedule.

In a dramatic twist from high school, my college peers almost instantaneously deemed me the smart one. I was frankly awestruck at how easy it was to convince everyone that I was smart. My grades lived up to my reputation. I soon became the resident homework helper. Group projects were never an issue because, unlike high school, most of my peers desired to be in my group, knowing that I would shoulder most of the work due to my perfectionism and desire to attend law school.

My professors, too, recognized my intellect in a new way, making securing accommodations with each individual professor seamless. Approximately one week before the beginning of each semester, I sent an introductory email to each professor, explaining who I was, my cerebral palsy, and requests for accommodations. Most of the time my reputation had already preceded me. I didn't anticipate organizing my own accommodations each semester, planning instead to go through the disability coordinator, a professor who wore many other hats as well. Yet after the first semester, my ability to work directly with professors became evident to all.

Self-coordination was simply more efficient for all. Accommodations included alternative test locations and extended test times so that I could adequately dictate answers to my scribe. These are the only accommodations I remember requesting during my undergraduate program. As I progressed through my program, my question switched from "Will I get into law school?" to "How much of a scholarship will I receive?" Obviously, I memorized the average admittance GPAs for both Nebraska law schools, so I became increasingly confident in my scholarship potential as I continued collecting As like a child collects rocks.

God working out accommodations was definitely His divine provision. As prepared as Mom and I tried to be when I entered college, there were many details that simply weren't worked out ahead of time. Looking back, I'm utterly shocked that I began the semester this way, but I didn't even know who my note taker in each class would be. When I walked into my first class, Old Testament Survey taught by my dear uncle John, I sat next to my second cousin, Katie. (Yes, many, many family members were associated with Grace.) Although Katie and I knew who each other were, we had never spoken prior to college. She offered to fill in the blanks in my note packet. Little did she know the door she was opening, as we had virtually every class together.

From then on, to the day we graduated from the business program, she selflessly assisted and took notes for me in every class. She was truly vital to my academic success and one of my biggest academic cheerleaders. She taught me so much about seeking the best for others above yourself. You see, she, too, was highly intelligent and could have easily felt competitive with me. Had she been like the Girls from high school, she would have definitely said, "I'm not helping you. You need to sink or swim on your own!" Yet competition was never a part of our relationship. Our commitment to friendship paid off, not only because we both performed exceptionally well academically, but also because to this day we count each other more as friends than distant relatives.

Not only did I receive straight As at Grace University, but also in my journalism co-op program with the University of Nebraska at Omaha. Although I ultimately graduated with a double major in business administration and biblical studies solely from Grace University, receiving multiple As from a state university gave more credibility to my high GPA. God may have used this stent at UNO to debunk questions of whether a sweet little Bible college actually made me earn my GPA. Even more credible is the fact that one semester I was simultaneously taking courses at four different colleges—Grace, UNO, and two online community colleges. All yielded the same results: As.

Why in the world would I take twenty four credit hours in one semester from four different institutions? Well, because I intended to triple major in journalism, business administration, and biblical studies until the registrar regretfully informed me that I could only receive two majors per degree. Although I was heartbroken to give up my journalism degree in order to avoid adding another year before law school, I'm now extremely thankful that I decided on the business administration degree. Little did I know then that I would be running my own business before the age of thirty! God knew. And He prepared me accordingly.

Even outside of academics, my popularity completely shifted from high school. I almost hate to use the word *popularity* because it has a snobby connotation. This wasn't so at Grace. The popular people were simply the people who were nice to everyone as opposed to people who everyone wanted to be. My range of friends was broad because high school taught me to be nice to everyone. As a result, there was never a shortage of friends to drive my van on late-night Walmart or McDonald's runs. In fact, friends quite preferred my van because of its seven-passenger capacity.

Another fun part of college was that the campus was located within walking distance of downtown and a beautiful park. I took countless walks both with friends and alone over my four years at Grace. The now more cautious Janae would likely be too nervous to walk alone given all of the potential unpredictable mishaps. However, even after witnessing a car accident literally six feet ahead on a street with no stoplight, the fearless college Janae was never deterred from her walks.

Given my outgoing personality, when I ran for student body association treasurer, almost no one but the other candidates were surprised. The fellow candidates hadn't yet gotten to know me. I was even able to win over my fellow candidates as soon as they read my speech. We would go on to be a dynamic team the next year. And I would be reelected as treasurer two more times, serving until I graduated. The student body president who I served with my first year—the one who was originally unsure about me—would go on to scare off potential treasurer candidates the next year on my behalf. When someone indicated an interest in running for treasurer, he quickly stated: "Well, Janae does that." I ran unopposed in my second and third elections.

Not all college was rosy, although looking back now after the hard times that were yet to come, it's difficult for me to see my dark days of college as anything more than slightly cloudy. True, I experienced my first heartbreak at age nineteen, followed by my first bout of depression. Yet I was constantly surrounded by friends that made even my saddest days fun. I was never lonely, despite having to come to grips with the fact that my cerebral palsy was the ultimate hindrance to me attracting the type of guy to which I was attracted. Still, as I sit and write this today, I feel fortunate that I experienced any small amount of true love before the horrors that awaited me in the years to come.

Facing my first depression, the melodrama of youth escalated the emotions. I wasn't actually medically depressed. I never saw a counselor or went on medication at that time. This is probably because not all hope was lost in my mind's eye. I clung to God, grew closer to Him, and prepared for my future career, which I faultily believed would bring ultimate fulfillment in life.

―――

As I shifted my focus from securing a husband to securing a full-ride scholarship to law school, my performance mentality drove me to new heights. From the time I was a college freshman, I followed a strict path-to-law-school checklist. This included visitations to the two law schools in Nebraska, requesting accommodations for the law school admissions test (LSAT), an LSAT prep course, and of course actually taking the LSAT and applying.

I was too insecure to request my own scribe for the LSAT, so I knew I would be dictating my answers to someone I didn't know and who was unfamiliar with my speech. The LSAT is intended to test logic and reading comprehension, not inherent legal knowledge. Most test takers utilize diagramming problems in the test booklet and highlighting key phrases in reading passages. I knew that, even with extended time, attempting to direct someone to draw a diagram that only made sense to me would be futile. Even trying to direct someone who was unfamiliar with my speech to highlight specific words would be more time consuming than it was worth. As a result, I spent six months learning how to visualize and complete the entire exam in my head. I learned every trick that I could to give me an edge. In this way, all that the scribe had to understand was A, B, C, D, or E. I would have plenty of time to correct any letters she heard incorrectly.

There was just one hiccup in my plan. The writing sample at the end of the exam, on which test takers were required to make a persuasive argument. My gift of writing would surely be hindered by my scribe's inability to understand my speech. I would have to use annoyingly simple words and short sentences, which wouldn't adequately convey my skills. There would simply not be enough time to spell a large number of words while still simultaneously crafting a writing sample masterpiece. I feared that my scholarship efforts would be thwarted by this last hurdle.

God again gave me the wisdom to minimize this disadvantage. Because Creighton University was my top choice for law school, I attended an open house a year prior to even taking the LSAT. I discussed my concerns about the writing sample portion of the LSAT with a professor and an admissions dean. I'd previously corresponded with both of them via email, so they were well aware of my writing abilities. They suggested that I keep the writing sample as concise as possible, but at the end note that I would be submitting a supplemental writing sample for the consideration of each law school's admissions committee.

This situation wasn't ideal, but the solution was the best I had.

I was forced to rely on God to open doors for not only law school scholarships, but law school admissions all together. When I sat for LSAT, I was relieved to find that my unknown test scribe was a kind older woman. She was sympathetic to my speech impediment concerns, and assisted me to the best of her abilities. As planned, I solved the majority of logic problems entirely in my head. I conducted the reading comprehension portion without making hardly any highlights or notes in the columns. When it came to the writing sample, I wrote a succinct paragraph, noting my speech impediment and that I would submit a secondary writing sample for consideration. The paragraph I wrote used simplistic logic to reach a basic conclusion to the question presented, showing that I did in fact have the ability to make a compelling argument on the spot, even if not robust or filled with complicated words due to my scribe's unfamiliarity with my speech.

My focus during the LSAT is best exemplified by the fact that every time I left the testing room for Mom to assist me in the bathroom, I turned the wrong way. It didn't matter if we were going toward or coming out of the bathroom—Mom had to point me in the right direction. My head was so in the test that I couldn't focus on anything else. Again, I couldn't be more grateful for Mom.

Weeks passed waiting for my test results. When they arrived, I received a score high enough to warrant me not going through this overly burdensome ordeal again. By my calculations, although not certain, my undergraduate GPA and LSAT score were sufficient to secure me a substantial scholarship at any of my top law school choices. Remember: proximity to family was the main consideration when evaluating law schools. Further, every article I read recommended attending law school where one wished to practice. As much as I would have loved to attend law school in the historic east coast or the tropical state of Hawaii, I knew I was more likely than not going to practice law in good ole Omaha, Nebraska. Prudence dictated that I attend law school in Nebraska, not only for the sake of caregiving by friends and family, but also to develop recognition and a network where I would eventually spend my career.

In typical Janae fashion, I secured recommendation letters and submitted law school applications as early as possible. The scholarship offers began rolling in soon thereafter. An online law school offered me a full-ride scholarship first. That night I received a voicemail from Dad asking me how it felt to earn $100,000. Following the online school, I received a full scholarship from a school in Des Moines, two hours from Omaha. Although exciting, the location wasn't ideal.

With every acceptance and offer, I became more confident in receiving a full-ride from Creighton University School of Law. I'll forever remember the day that the big white envelope came. I was home at my parents for Thanksgiving. Praise God, because I don't think it would have been possible for Mom to wait to open the envelope longer than it took for her to run in house, yell my name, and throw the envelope on the counter. She helped me tear open the envelope, folding open the embordered folder that was inside. She patiently waited for me to read the letter.

First—congratulations on your acceptance. Sort of anticlimactic for us both because we already knew my credentials undoubtedly warranted acceptance.

Then I read the next part. Although I don't recall the exact language, tears filled my eyes as I informed Mom that I, her daughter who had graduated high school in the middle of the pack, had worked hard enough to receive a full scholarship plus a textbook stipend to Creighton University School of Law.

Mom quickly lifted me into a truck so that we could drive to where Dad was chopping wood on the back acres of our land. The window was open on my passenger side. As soon as we drove up, I flashed the big white envelope out the window at him. He ran over, saying, "You got in!" When we told him that I also received the scholarship offer, he wiped tears from his eyes, saying, "Praise God! I'm so proud of you!"

From that day on, as far as undergrad went, the pressure was off. Although my pride continued to compel me to earn As, I easily finished the last few weeks of my senior fall semester and eagerly headed into my final semester of nine credit hours. I'd worked hard for three and a half years, so I was going to soak up all of the friendships and spiritual growth I could in my final semester. Although there was no way for me to know the hardships and horrors that law school would bring, something in me told me that I needed to take in all of the spiritual strength and wisdom possible for the road ahead. So I soaked up every spiritual teaching that Grace University offered, attending chapels and Bible studies like never before. I even attended some Bible classes that I wasn't enrolled in, just to take in all of the wisdom possible before my reentry into the real world.

As most good things in life, my last semester at Grace University eventually came to an end. I'm grateful that I was still optimistic about the life that law school would bring. Had I not been, my departure from Grace would have been infinitely sadder than it already was. I wasn't only leaving behind a safe environment of faculty and staff, but also living with all of my closest friends. I took solace in knowing that one of my closest friends was going to be my roommate and other Grace friends would continue to be caregivers. This was only possible because, by some miraculous twist, God ordained that Grace University would only be a mere minutes' drive from Creighton University.

Still, as me and my closest classmate took turns going to the baccalaureate stage to accept the most prestigious awards offered by the college, I couldn't fight the sinking feeling in my stomach that it was downhill from here.

Enjoy this, Janae, I told myself. *You are about to go from being a big fish in a little pond to being a little fish in a big pond. You know the image you worked so hard to create for yourself here? Congratulations, you are about to have to do it all over at Creighton, not with aspiring pastors or teachers, but with aspiring lawyers and congressmen. Yes, soak in all these accolades because they are about to go silent.*

Law School

Buckle up. We're headed into the darkest, dampest tunnel of my life thus far. This unforgivingly bumpy ride lasted from Tuesday, June 4, 2013, at 8:00 a.m. through Saturday, February 27, 2016, at noon. Two years, eight months, twenty-three days, and four hours. Alternatively: 142 weeks; 998 days; 23,956 hours; 1,437,360 minutes; or 86,241,600 seconds of sheer challenge and turmoil. I'm wary of describing any part of my life as horrible, as I know there are so many people who go through much more horror than I'll ever experience. How can anyone's trials compare to those faced by Corrie Ten Boom in the Nazi concentration camp or by starving African children sold into sex slavery?

Bearing in mind that I'll likely never face hardships as great as these, law school was my horror. Even being steadfastly convinced that God ordained me for law school, I don't know if I would be able to choose to go through the fires of this stone institution again. My perspective was skewed. My friendships were tested. My family was blindsided. My faith was depleted. My sanity was lost. My will to live was gone. I see God's grace in these moments in that He sustained me and allowed me to continue to impact people for His glory. I see His grace in that I didn't end my life—no matter how much I wanted to.

Be warned: this is not pretty.

Day one.

Naive is not the correct word to describe how I entered the metal doors of the concrete law building. Ironically, the law school building had an appearance comparable to the experience that awaited beyond its heavy doors. But for the windows lining the second of the two floors, the building looked about as similar to a prison as you can get. No artistic architecture was used. In the days to come, the rectangular concrete sign at the entrance, reading "Creighton University School of Law," would constantly look like the headstone that I imagined would mark my grave. Of course, on day one, the appearance of the law school looked more modern and academic to me than oppressive and bleak.

I say I wasn't naive because I'd probably done as much research on law school over the past two years as anyone could. I read all of the books, spoke to many attorneys and professors, and even attended a law school admissions conference in Chicago. Although the Chicago trip was a fun girl's getaway with Mom and my sister, Julie, the conference was essentially unhelpful because I'd already read all the materials.

I wasn't naive. I was prepared, armed with a full-ride and textbook scholarship along with the undergrad academic awards received just two weeks prior. *This will be a challenge, but nothing I can't handle*, I confidently thought. After all, 90 percent of the classes were graded strictly on the final exam. *My undergrad GPA and LSAT score far exceeds the average for students entering Creighton, and I'm good at cramming, so I can beat the curve and do decently well.* Confidence. Grace University had given me confidence that I carried proudly as I wheeled through the law school doors with my head held high, ready to take on anything.

Well, not anything. Not this. By the end of day one, my doe-eyed excitement for law school turned into a deer-in-the-headlights panic. The stares—I'd forgotten about the stares. After spending four years in an environment comparable to Frodo's shire in Lord of the Rings, when I left the safe warm bubble of Grace University, I experienced reentrance shock. It's not that I'd gone four years without being stared at, but when I was, I was usually surrounded by people who loved me. As new classes would enter Grace University, the upperclassmen would almost instantly take it upon themselves to inform the newbies of my intelligence and wit. This relay of information would result in rapid acceptance by my new peers, such that the wary looks and stares would be almost unnoticeable year after year.

Not so at law school. I was completely alone that day. My friend Mariah selflessly accepted a position as my assistant for the summer so that I could enter the accelerated juris doctorate program. Mariah would pick me up from my parents' house at 7:15 a.m. to drive me a half hour to law school. Except for intervals of free time, while I was in class, she would work until 9:00 p.m., five days a week. I'd elected to complete the accelerated juris doctorate program to avoid a summer gap in my resume. Finding a worthwhile summer job for the interim between undergrad and law school wasn't possible given the accommodations that would have to be made for me to perform any job. Figuring out accommodations for my physical limitations was simply not worth the hassle in light of the fact that I would only be working the job for about ten weeks.

Mariah dropped me off for my first 8:00 a.m. class, but didn't go inside with me. This is why I was completely alone in the sea of puzzling looks as my wheelchair weaved through the onlookers.

"What is she doing here?"

"Is she in the right building?"

"How did she get accepted into this program?"

These are just some of the words I associated with the stares from everyone, from the janitor to the librarians. I could have been misreading their faces, but, accurate or not, my initial nerves began to tremble more and more with each person I passed.

When I entered the classroom, I encountered the same students who had been at orientation. Orientation didn't scare me, because, as I already said, I read all of the books possible prior to even orientation. As I entered the classroom, I elected to sit in the back by the student who appeared the least intimidating. His name was John—a Mormon with a growing family. He was already aware of my situation because the law school had asked him to be my notetaker for the summer. John was instantly friendly, beginning an encouraging friendship that lasted throughout law school. I feel blessed that God had given me someone I could talk to during the dozens of hours in the building.

Notes—the first emotional test for which I was unprepared. In undergrad, the notes were either fill in the blank or unimportant because the information was in the textbook. As long as I secured a notetaker reliable enough to accurately fill in the blanks, I didn't need to worry about writing down additional material. In law school, there were no fill in the blanks. Further, it became quickly apparent from day one that the professors loved to talk about material outside of the textbooks.

This sent me into a panic. I looked around the classroom, seeing other students ferociously writing as the professor spoke. I tried to type on my iPad with my nose in shorthand just in case John missed a key point. However, typing with my nose was almost entirely futile because I fell too far behind due to my typing speed. Once I realized how behind I was, I panicked, even more, worrying that I missed something that the professor had said.

I'm not sure whether I burst into tears with Mariah for the first time on day one or day two. Either way, I was confident that I wasn't going to pass law school. Adding even more pressure was the local news story that was released on the day I began law school.

> Mom: One of the purposes of weddings is accountability so everyone knows—more pressure not to quit.
> Me: Ok ...?
> Mom: You're now married to law school because it was on TV. Now you can't quit.
> Me: Good analogy, Mom?
> —June 5, 2013

Mom had the best intentions, but her statement made me feel that there was no way out. I could never quit law school unless I failed out because everyone was watching me. I needed to keep inspiring people, so I needed to keep going.

Note all of the I's in those statements. My view of God's plan and grace was underdeveloped at this point. I should have realized that it wasn't up to me. God was in charge of my life—whether I failed or succeeded at law school. If I would have consistently rejected the lie that my future was all on me, I would have saved myself a lot of heartache and depression. Oh, how we hurt ourselves when we don't trust God to orchestrates our lives the way He sees fit.

Given that the Holy Spirit was at work in me, I did have a few moments of clarity during those early days of law school. This clarity allowed me to decide that I would stick it out and see how I did on the first round of finals. I honestly didn't care if I failed. Then I wouldn't have to do this anymore. The chatter of my peers before and after class made me feel as if I was the dumbest person in the room.

Even in the midst of my doubts stemming from my inability to take notes and clearly speak, I found ways to work my disability in my favor. Most importantly, I realized that professors were reluctant to call on me out of fear that they would be embarrassed when they couldn't understand me. If they did call on me, the questions were usually yes or no hypotheticals. This pattern of questioning deviated from the usual Socratic method used to humiliate law students.

For those of you unfamiliar with law school, the Socratic method is a way of teaching students by asking questions to encourage critical thinking. The basis for these questions is the assigned cases for any given class. Here is the catch though: with the exception of constitutional law, the facts of any given case are largely irrelevant to the final exam. Stick with me here. The final exams were based upon knowledge of the legal principles applied in the cases. Essentially, we were given a factual scenario and graded on how well we applied the law. So because I'm not a person who needs examples to understand principles, the facts of the cases were irrelevant to my performance on the final.

Remember: law school grades are based solely on final exams. Free from the worry of being embarrassed with the Socratic method, I barely focused on the facts of the cases. Whereas some students would spend hours briefing cases (aka summarizing) to prepare for class, I only focused on outlining and memorizing the legal principles. When I received the notes from John, I would integrate them into my outline—based on what I predicted the professor would use on the final. The amount of time this approach saved me was invaluable. Even though I still studied close to seventy hours per week, my study time wasn't wasted on anything that wouldn't impact my GPA and class rank. After all, future employers would see my GPA and class rank, not whether I knew the facts of a random case in a textbook.

Once Mariah and I got our outlining system down, we worked like a well-oiled machine. I was still overwhelmed, but my goal was simply to see how I performed on summer finals. I wasn't thinking long term. To my utter surprise, I received the highest grade in all three of my summer classes. I wasn't the only one who was surprised. One day, the most intimidating girl in our summer class was bragging about how she got the second-highest grade. She desperately wanted to know who scored higher than her. I wasn't about to tell her. However, John knew me too well.

"Was it you?" he asked with a smile. I couldn't lie, so I tried to quietly tell him yes. He exclaimed, "Great job!" When the intimidating girl heard, the look of astonishment on her face was priceless. I feared I now had a target on my back.

With the summer semester under my belt, I eagerly moved into my first apartment with my dear college friend, Amber. We were both extremely excited to make this two-bedroom, two-bathroom downtown apartment our home. I only had a week in between semesters, but we made the most of it. She loved to cook, which was a blessing in the months to come. Unfortunately, by the time I moved out of those apartments at the end of law school, the walls would feel more like a padded room of an insane asylum than a home.

Based on how well I did my first semester, you would think that my second semester would have an easier beginning. Not so. I experienced my first overt disability discrimination in the weeks to follow. In undergrad, I would begin each semester by emailing all of my professors prior to the first class, explaining my disability. I found that this proactive approach helped ease their nerves. All of my undergrad professors indicated that they appreciated and understood my intelligence despite my physical limitations.

In law school, I took a slightly different approach, knowing that law school professors were renowned for being temperamental and unpredictable. Aware that the law school administration likely explained my condition to my professors already, I waited until after the first class to determine if an introductory email was necessary. I gauged the necessity of an email from their initial facial expressions and interactions with me.

I didn't have time to email one professor before he called me into his office. "What are you doing here?" he asked without batting an eye. My faithful assistant, Ella, was with me to interpret my speech. I explained that I planned to be a research attorney.

"Well, we will just have to do the best we can then." He went on to say that he couldn't call on me in class, so he wanted me to take notes on all of the readings and email them to him every day. "I need to make sure you get it." My explanation that I'd been number one over the summer semester didn't change his mind. In fact, he looked at me as if I was exaggerating my academic performance. I was so taken aback by his treatment of me that I simply agreed to his proposal and left his office as quickly as possible.

When I recounted the events to my parents in tears, they didn't let me use his words as an excuse to give up. I told them, "See? People are always going to think I can't be an attorney, even if I earn perfect grades." My wise parents, in line with their usual behavior, reiterated that I can't let people define me. Dad, who rarely swears, may have used a curse word or two to describe the professor. Then he beseeched me to prove him wrong.

After consulting with John, my classmate notetaker, and some of my other law school friends about my unfair predicament, I decided to go to the academic dean. Even though I took notes about everything I read anyway, as I explained earlier, my notes were only geared toward the final exam. I knew the professor wouldn't be satisfied with my notes, as they were devoid of case-specific facts. Further, given that the notes were for my studying only, I didn't correct the grammar or spelling of my scribes. There simply wasn't enough time in a day. Essentially, if I would have sent my notes, he would have found me as incompetent as he believed I was. I wasn't going to waste valuable time polishing my notes for him, only to do worse on finals. Again, my GPA and class rank were my only priorities.

When I talked to the academic dean, he thankfully understood my reasoning. The academic dean had been one of my professors over the summer, so he knew that calling on me in class was indeed possible even if the questions needed to be asked differently to allow for simple and understandable responses. Thus, I also reinforced that I was more than willing to answer any questions in class. John and other friends would have gladly interpreted for the professor. However, I was simply unwilling to do more work than the average just because the professor took a unique issue with my disability. The academic dean promptly informed the professor of the situation. He never called on me in class.

During my last semester of law school, I elected to take a night class with the same professor. Although I still detested him, having all of my classes on two days was more important to me than avoiding him. He again discriminated against me. This time he was more cunning. He went to the new academic dean and explained that I wouldn't be able to participate in the group project because of my speech impediment. The group project was to negotiate a settlement with another group. The professor proposed to the academic dean that I review and critique the recorded negotiations instead of participating as a group member. I didn't fight this ridiculous proposal. At this point, I already had a job offer to be an associate attorney at my firm. Frankly, it was easier to critique the negotiations than be in them. I had very little fire left in me at this time in law school. I just wanted to graduate. Had I possessed the fire I have today, I would have never settled for being excluded from the group.

I wonder what he would think if he knew that I have participated in three negotiations to the present date—one which settled for a hefty confidential sum.

≈

Not all professors were discriminatory. Most were my biggest advocates as I looked for employment. When asked for recommendations, they were eager to rave about my intelligence and ability to overcome adversity. One of my favorite law school professors wasn't liked by most students. He was generally known to be hard-nosed. However, I found favor with him from day one. As soon as he read my first email to him, he knew I was highly intelligent. He also respected my no-nonsense work ethic. He would frequently give me hypotheticals in front of the class, being impressed whenever he was unable to trick me.

One time, when another professor was unwilling to give me the accommodations I needed, he fought for me until the other professor understood why my requests were equitable. Namely, in the final for the class, the professor allowed us to bring one page of notes along with everything we could write in our textbook. However, the professor didn't understand why I needed to be allowed to bring in more typed notes than other students in light of the fact that I couldn't physically write in my textbook. Directing my scribes to write in my book would have required them to type each phrase before they wrote it to ensure no written errors in the book. My favorite professor recognized that this process would be unbearably tedious and detract from the actual learning of the material. Thankfully, he was able to explain to the professor that allowing me to print out the notes that the average student would write in the textbook was the only equitable approach.

My favorite professor's admiration for me was confirmed at my hooding ceremony, when he broke decorum to give me a hug on stage, exclaiming, "You were always my favorite!"

So, did I graduate number one? Nope. When my class size increased from about a dozen to about 135 following the first summer semester, I gave up my hopes of being number one. I fell into the worst depression of my life during law school. Some days I didn't do any homework. Some days I skipped class. Most days I went to class and found comfort in iPad games. Playing these games was the only way I felt I could avoid becoming unbearably overwhelmed by the sound of note-taking and eloquent speeches by my peers.

I operated in a fog. But God—He was there in the fog. As many times as I disengaged from school, He gave me the strength and will to reengage with all the more vigor the next day. He kept me from engaging in regular drinking, unlike most of my classmates. This meant that on Saturday mornings, I was ready for a nine-hour day of studying with no hangover deficits. He also used my disability to make sure I got enough sleep to be alert and on my mental game. Even though I woke up at 6:00 a.m. on most weekdays, I would be in bed at 9:00 p.m. essentially every night. This was the time my caregivers left. There was no point continuing to type or study without them, given my slow typing speed. After mindlessly watching one episode of *7th Heaven*, I would easily fall asleep from exhaustion.

Beyond my own fog, another obstacle of law school was finding efficient scribes. Not all caregivers make excellent scribes. Further, typing for me in law school was infinitely more difficult than in undergrad. The difficulty stemmed from the fact that we were only typing study notes. One would think typing study notes would be easier than papers. On the contrary. My study notes needed to be abbreviated as much as possible so I could efficiently memorize content for the finals. In addition to legal terms, I was also trying to dictate abbreviations, making my scribe's job significantly more difficult.

I also needed scribes to assist me with finals. The average final for the typical law student lasted three hours. Almost every law student will attest that every minute allotted was necessary to write the most encompassing essay possible. I received the reasonable accommodation of double time, which meant that I had to complete the finals within six uninterrupted hours. I think that my scribes and I allotted ourselves one bathroom break during the six hours. In case any of my former peers are reading this book, before you become jealous of my extended time, remember my speech is labored and slow. On top of that, the scribes had to understand my speech well enough to type the essays. Further, as I dictated, I also simultaneously edited the scribe's spelling and grammar. Comparing this to the ability to type at least sixty words per minute by oneself with inherently correct grammar and spelling, double time was arguably no advantage at all.

Despite all of my struggles in law school, God allowed me to graduate number 15 out of 122 students. In order to achieve grades good enough for this feat, I had to forgo all extracurricular activities and focus solely on my grades. Whereas a Janae without a disability would have likely heeded the advice to join law review, I knew that I couldn't handle another responsibility on top of studying for my classes and managing my caregivers. For those of you who are lay people, law review is revered as the most prestigious activity for a law student. On law review, students write and edit published legal articles. Those in the top third of the class, as I was, are invited to write on to law review, which essentially means try out. I simply couldn't handle the additional time commitment while attempting to maintain high grades.

The trials didn't end when I graduated. I still had one more hurdle to overcome on my journey to become an attorney. The dreaded bar exam. I once again had to request accommodations, which involved submitting doctor's notes and documentation of every educational accommodation since elementary school. Further, the specificity to which I had to request accommodations was uncanny. For example, I forgot to request permission to bring in a straw so I could drink water. Had it not been for the graciousness of the director, I would have had to go through the whole five-day bar exam without drinking water. Most test takers take the exam in two days, but with how the exam sections had to be divided to accommodate double time, one section had to be completed on the morning of the fifth day. It was definitely a marathon and not a sprint, continuing to review my study materials every evening after a day of testing as not to lose any knowledge over the five days. I had no appetite. Mom bought me a whole caramel apple pie for dinner one night just to entice me to eat more.

My cerebral palsy even got in the way of applying to take the bar exam. My hand was too unsteady to use the electronic fingerprinting machine to obtain the required fingerprints to be admitted to the Nebraska Bar. Thankfully, the police officers at the precinct were nice enough to use old-fashioned ink, but even this process was a challenge given the precise boxes and positions that the fingerprints had to be in.

When all was said and done, I was approved to take the bar exam. However, studying was another hurdle. The excitement of graduating a semester early in December was quickly replaced by the anxiety of studying every day for the eight weeks preceding the exam. The first day of studying resulted in a sobbing phone call to my parents, telling them that I just couldn't do it. In the ultimate display of tough love, Dad told me to knock it off and do it. Somehow, I relied on God for strength to persevere through those eight weeks of studying. During those eight weeks, I also moved from my starter apartment by the law school to an apartment on the other side of town where my pending job was located. I barely remember packing or unpacking, as Mom, Dad, my grandma, and two of my aunts did essentially everything for me as I studied.

By the time of the first day of the bar exam, I was as much of a robot machine as I'd ever been. My mind was packed full of knowledge, and my focus was uncanny. My assistant Kersten and I drove one hour to the location of the bar exam. I would make this drive for the next five days. I desperately needed Kersten to help me with every essay section of the exam because she was by far the most skilled at spelling, grammar, and fast typing. Yet on day five, neither of us remembered whether "defendant" was spelled "-ant" or "-ent." Although I paid her a fair amount, she selflessly arrived at my apartment at 6:00 a.m. on all three essay days of the exam. We would do a three-hour session in the morning, have an hour break, and do another three-hour session in the afternoon before driving an hour back home.

I said my focus was uncanny. On day one of the exam, when we arrived in the parking lot of the testing center, the rickety door of my fourteen-year-old van fell off. I was almost completely unfazed by this. I called Mom and said quite matter-of-factly, "My van door fell off. Deal with it. I'm going in." I'm not normally this demanding when I ask for help, but when you are about to take the most important test of your life, pleasantries go out the window. My amazing mother drove the hour to the testing center, evaluated the situation, and rented me a handicapped-accessible van for the rest of the exam.

Little did I know that on that very day my grandparents were driving my new handicapped-accessible Honda Element back from Florida. My parents had graciously provided all my siblings with a relatively new vehicle when they graduated high school. However, given handicapped-accessible vehicles are so expensive, when I graduated high school, I got the seven-year-old family accessible minivan. Although nice for hauling the maximum number of college students on McDonald's runs, by the time I was done with law school, I was ready for a new vehicle. I needed a new vehicle. My parents again graciously provided me with the Honda Element that was virtually unused. Not only was this vehicle sportier than the minivan, but I could finally sit in the front passenger seat. My parents and in-town siblings came over to surprise me with the vehicle on the day I finished the bar exam. I don't think I have ever been so surprised in my life.

During the multiple-choice sections of the exam, my assistant Janelle helped fill in the bubbles. She, too, would arrive at my apartment early in the morning to make the one-hour drive. Of any of my assistants or caregivers, Janelle probably endured the most. Janelle was the one who helped me full-time during my last semester of law school and while I studied for the bar exam. By God's grace and forgiveness on both our parts, we're friends today.

At this point in my life, my anger and lack of patience was at an all-time high. Spending forty hours per week with someone is difficult when you're in a good emotional place, testing even the closest of relationships. When one party is severely emotionally depleted, it's next to impossible. For example, Janelle would do something as simple as suggest a different place to store my soda in my new apartment, and it would irritate me to no end. My need for absolute unquestioned control over little things likely stemmed from my life feeling completely out of control in every other area. The way I treated Janelle is even sadder considering that she agreed to start working full time at a moment's notice when I was in a real jam my last semester of law school. I thank God for providing Janelle for those six months.

After six excruciating weeks of waiting for the results that would tell me whether or not law school had all been in vain, and whether or not I would lose my coveted job offer, I received news that I'd indeed passed with a large margin. However, my emotional turmoil and internal struggles with faith and life were far from over.

Part Four

INTERNAL STRUGGLES

Dark Days

Depression. More people struggle with it than we would like to admit. Some hide it. Some use it as a crutch. Some, who have never struggled with the dark depths, merely minimize depression's existence in the lives of others.

Writing about the severity of my depression is not easy. Truth be told, I've been staring at this blank chapter for months, trying to put darkness into eloquent, but honest, words is unbelievably difficult. As I type this chapter, I sit in my childhood bedroom, where I always felt safe, not only from the evil outside these walls, but also from the inner turmoil of my heart. The turmoil of depression may have still been present at times in this cozy bedroom, but the love that has surrounded me while I'm in this house seems to crush it back into the recesses of my mind.

Next to me is my faithful caregiver, Anna, someone whom I know is emotionally strong enough to type the difficult words that I'm about to dictate. After all, she was with me through what I believe was my rock bottom.

So, how does God fit into my depression? Why would a

woman of lifelong faith go through such mental and spiritual anguish? I have come to realize that mental pain is similar to physical pain. As a result of a fallen world, some of us will suffer from mental pain and disability, but if we allow Him, God can redeem it for His glory. Just as I can find joy amidst my physical disability of cerebral palsy, I can find joy amidst depression.

Hearing of physically disabled individuals struggling with depression is not uncommon. However, I feel that I didn't truly struggle with depression until my early twenties. Sure, there was the dramatic college heartbreak I weathered. But I believe that this painful season of my life was different from my years of depression for one simple reason—not all hope was lost in my mind's eye. Although heartbroken, I sincerely believed I would find love within the next few years. It wasn't until I began law school at age twenty-two that I became truly depressed in the medical sense of the word.

The difference between my seven-year depression and other sad times in my life is glaring—this time I was utterly hopeless. I felt trapped in a life I didn't choose or want anymore. I felt that cerebral palsy limited my career options to the point where law school was my only option. After all, but for earning an attorney's salary, how would I pay for my assistants? Moreover, the pressure was unbearable. If I wasn't at the top of my class, who would hire a severely disabled woman?

Looking around at other Christian women my age, I saw many marrying men who worked hard to provide for their young brides. Why had God not afforded me the same luxury? Why was I putting in twelve-hour days to try to make a living for myself when others could rely upon their husbands? As much as I fought to adopt the feminist mindset of being a powerful woman, the deepest part of my soul simply longed to be loved and taken care of by a man.

The result of all of these feelings was hopelessness and distrust of God. After following Him all of my life, I wrongly felt entitled to my long-imagined white picket fence life—the one with a suit-wearing husband, two kids, a dog, and two cats. The one in which I would spend my days caring for my children and cooking for my family. Dinner would be at six o'clock every night and we would come to church in our Sunday best every week.

Instead, I was fighting through law school, handling all the judgmental looks, sometimes rude professors, and academic pressures on my own. Of course, looking back now I recognize that marriage and kids aren't the answer to life's problems. I can say with absolute integrity that if God's will is for me to be single, then I'll be the happiest single. I also see that I wasn't on my own. Not for one day. Not for one moment. In addition to the Holy Spirit propelling me forward through every challenge, God had given me friends and family to walk beside me down this undeniably difficult road.

Moments of clarity led to brief glimpses of these truths, but most moments for the better part of seven years were dark and gray. In law school I would consistently wake up and bemoan the fact that I hadn't died in my sleep. Then, I would angrily thrust my feet to the floor and pull on my headboard to get up and start another day.

You know those movie scenes where the main character is walking around in a fog of muffled voices? That is how I felt every day when I entered the law school building. I know that I somehow smiled at people, because people thought I was friendly. But for the life of me, I could never understand why anyone was smiling in that godforsaken building. The fog followed me day in and day out for months.

This is not how my life was supposed to go. Eventually, I would fantasize about ending my life by driving my wheelchair off one of the long cement staircases I passed on my way to and from school. My apartment was close enough for me to walk, so I frequently wheeled to and from class alone. Imagine a person in wet, baggy clothes shuffling through thick mire, that is the feeling I had on every trip.

When I began law school, I began attending a new church plant in my area of town. As I mentioned before, during college, I began attending a megachurch with my college friends. Although I never connected at the church, I didn't feel a real need to because I lived in the fellowship of Bible college each day and attended chapel four days a week. During Bible college years, church attendance was more for the purpose of developing the healthy habit of regular fellowship rather than vital weekly encounters with God and other believers.

However, I knew that I needed to find a smaller church when I began law school. I had such high hopes for this smaller church plant to become my permanent church family. Alas, the church plant quickly grew and I soon found myself feeling lost in a sea of faces. Church attendance once again was just something I did. My affection and trust for God was at an all-time low, so church felt more religious than ever. When I say "religious," I mean I was "doing religion" in the way that many people outside the church view Christians. It was something I did every Sunday morning to keep my parents happy. It was strictly a ritual without any relationship with God or others.

A well-meaning mentor told me that I needed to spend an hour with God every day. I thought, *Lady, if I had an extra hour each day, I would sleep more.* Still, the lack of priority I placed on my relationship with God is likely one of the reasons that I fell into a deep depression. Note that I said one of the reasons. When I left undergrad, I felt the most spiritually strong I'd ever been thus far in my life. This is where I think we must recognize mental health in the context of a fallen world. It only took a few months of law school to completely break my spirits. Looking back, there are certain behaviors I could have done differently. For example, spending more time with God beyond desperate and angry prayers. Still, if I endured law school all over again, I hardly think my mental health would be much better.

Explaining this to you, my reader, is unbelievably difficult. How do I explain surviving one of the hardest academic programs with one of the most severe physical disabilities? For me, it felt like I was trapped in a stone room with a pick. I know that all of the other students are trapped in similar rooms with the same pick. However, they can more effectively pound the pick with the hammer in search of water. I, on the other hand, drop the hammer with every swing I attempt. My body hurts like never before. Given that there is only one final at the end of the semester for each class, none of us are even sure we're digging in the right direction for water. Yet we all must keep swinging. Day after day. Minute after minute. Everyone can see that I drop my hammer after every swing, causing me immense humiliation like I never experienced before.

In anger, I cry to God to get me out of this prison. My ears only hear my words echoing off the stone walls. I look up through the steel-barred windows to my parents, saying, "Can't you get me out of here!"

They respond with encouragement to keep fighting, asking what my other plan would be.

"I don't know! I just want out!" I cry.

My friends also encourage me to keep going, reminding me of how much I have overcome and how smart I am.

"If I quit, I let them down too," I tell myself.

I felt I couldn't quit. I'd never quit before. Illogically, I felt that if I quit law school, I would prove everyone who thought I would never amount to anything right. I just couldn't choose to quit. Thus, the only way for me to get out of law school is to create a situation where I had no choice but to quit.

Two prior experiences with cutting my wrist on the surface had taught me that I lacked the nerve to make deep enough cuts to do any real damage. Both cutting episodes had stemmed from the same root problem that I wouldn't recognize until age twenty-seven—my prideful perfectionism: *if I can't do it perfectly, I don't want to do it at all.* The first time occurred after one of the biggest fights with my parents. I was a dramatic sixteen-year-old who felt like a complete failure merely because I failed to obey their entertainment and computer guidelines. No damage was done but looking back now I roll my eyes at my immature self. The second cutting was a tad less trivial, occurring when I was nineteen years old as I came to grips with the ending of a relationship with the only man I have ever romantically loved to this day. Then, too, I was simply trying to find a distraction from my mistakes in the relationship.

Perfectionism. The thought process that led to my 2013 overdose wasn't overly complex. If I couldn't do law school perfectly, I didn't want to do it at all, but to quit was to fail in my eyes. Yes, there again in my gray apartment I was facing my personal demon of perfectionism. I needed to quit, not by choice but by medical necessity. Cutting was far too dangerous to accomplish the desired result. This left few options, given my alcohol and drug-free home. Ibuprofen. That is what I had. That is what I could open. You may think I premeditated this plan for weeks, days, or at least a few hours. No, I made this decision in a matter of minutes. One of my best friends, Stephanie, had just left my apartment after getting me up and ready for class. She was on her way to chapel at the Bible college I'd just left a few months prior. See, even the placement of my law school within a five-minute drive from my undergrad Bible college was God's grace so that my friends could continue to work as caregivers for me during law school.

As much evidence of God's grace that surrounded me, thankfulness wasn't on my mind as my weary eyes gazed back at me from my bathroom mirror. Fight-or flight sensations came over me as I knew I simply couldn't bear to walk back into the harsh law school building one more time. Within a matter of minutes, I knocked the ibuprofen bottle from its shelf, opened it, and swallowed as many tiny, reddish, round pills as I could without throwing them back up.

When the reality of what I'd done quickly set in, I called Stephanie right away. The amount of desperate phone calls Stephanie has received since that day is a true testament to her committed friendship. Some people object to saying that depressed people are often selfish. I don't. Whether I intend to be or not, in the deepest depths of my depression I'm inherently selfish. If I'm unable to even treat myself well on my darkest days, how can I comprehend that my actions are hurting the ones I love the most, like Stephanie.

True to her character, Stephanie answered. Upon hearing what I'd done, she recruited another friend, Ella, to rush me to the ER. How I didn't think she would call Mom is beyond me. Mom arrived at the ER shortly after I was admitted. I was embarrassed to have the doctors and nurses know that I'd willingly overdosed on ibuprofen, but above all else, I was still in a depressed fog. I choked down the activated charcoal, which my parents took as a positive sign that I still had the will to live. In my head, I thought, *I just don't have the will to fight against instructions.*

Did I want to die? I continue to ask myself this question about my overdose to this day. It is difficult to understand a mind so twisted with depression. I think, at the very least, I was apathetic to whether I lived or died. Undeniably, I wanted out of life as I was currently living it.

I remember moments of my stay in the ICU in slow motion scenes. I only remember Dad's anger, probably simply because he wanted so badly to fix my life. He had to leave an important meeting to come to the hospital right away. I remember Mom's sadness, as she called my two closest aunts. I remember being interviewed by psychiatric residents, thinking, *I know the right answers to give you to all of these questions.* When my little brother and sister came to visit me, I remember a flood of shameful embarrassment. True to their character, Jeffrey tried to offer a few wise words of encouragement and Julie brought me candy to try to lift my spirits.

Above all else, I remember being relieved that I had no option but to lie there in the ICU bed. I couldn't study for the first time in months. Relief from law school was all I sought. I let my mind drift into the fog of nothingness, reflecting on disjointed scenes from my life thus far. I prayed but don't remember the content of the prayers other than that my words were tainted with feelings of anger and betrayal toward God. Finally, I remember thinking of how disappointed Jamison, my older brother in med school at the time, must be with me. *This seals it*, I thought, *I'm officially the black sheep of the family.*

Unsurprisingly, given that I'd displayed no symptoms, I spent only one night in the ICU. I was supposed to go to regular counseling. I was supposed to look into antidepressants. Notwithstanding a few sessions with the free counseling service provided at my law school, I followed through with neither recommendation.

I was back in class the same week, living as if nothing had happened. It is beyond me how I managed to continue effectively studying. No doubt this is due to the Lord's strength. Although

Moments of Grace

I still prayed throughout the next two and a half years, I pretty much told God that I would see Him on the other side of law school. In my anger, confusion, and depression, I didn't want to contribute anything to my relationship with Him. *He got me into this mess. He gave me this awful life-limiting disability. He can wait a few years while I try to survive.*

Yet even as I struggled internally with my faith, I tried to be a godly example and encouragement to others. Knowing that I would eventually return to the ultimate lover of my soul, being a good Christian was part of my autopilot lifestyle along with being a good student. *Woe to me if I cause others to struggle with their faith just because I can't get it together.* With the Holy Spirit still at work in my life, I was still able to pen Facebook posts evidencing some amount of spiritual wisdom.

I settled into my new sad normal. I earned good grades. I secured the coveted Union Pacific clerkship. I even hoped that post-law school would bring a better life. There were still moments of laughter with friends and joy with family. Others' lives continued to move on all around me. Weddings happened, and so did breakups. Family vacations occurred as they always did. My first nephews were even born (twins!). I was present for all of these changes with all of these loved ones—well, as much as I could be in my depressed autopilot state.

Then, the unthinkable happened. It's the type of tragedy that you never think will happen to you. You read about it. You hear about it. You even watch stories depicting its horror. But, deep down, you don't believe it will ever happen to you. Until it does, no matter how educated and careful you think you are.

I was raped.

When I began this book, I didn't intend to include this part of my story. I intended, and still intend, to write an entirely separate book devoted to helping Christian women work through the trauma of being raped. However, for purposes of authenticity, I couldn't omit such a life-altering event from this book.

I didn't know how to explain the rape and the implications cohesively until I was able to paint. Allow me a brief moment to detail the journey to achieving the ability to even paint at all. Understandably, if I'm unable to even write with a pen, my painting ability had previously been severely limited. Mom, being the enthusiastic champion of mine that she is, allowed me to paint, an extremely messy activity that only ever achieved a messy product. As I grew older, and my perfectionistic tendencies developed, painting became less and less fun. I couldn't even place one mark where I intended it to go, aggravating me to no end. We tried many different methods, including taping the paintbrush to my hand or holding the paintbrush in my mouth. None of these methods left me satisfied with my end creation. I hung up my artistic aspirations for good when I was just a child.

This past year, one of my caregivers, Becca, offered to assist me in trying to paint by placing an elastic headband on my head to secure a paintbrush to my forehead. Being an occupational therapy student, she waited almost two years before trying out any of her techniques on me. This is a testament to her sensitivity and ability to read the situation and specific needs of disabled individuals. When I repeatedly began to voice a deep longing to paint, she suggested the headband. I skeptically agreed to try it with little hope that it would work.

To my complete astonishment, I was actually able to place the stroke where I intended the paint to go. The feeling was a relief that I have never experienced before. The healing of expressing myself without words was indescribable. Emotions bled from the paintbrush without need for explanation. At the beginning of a painting, my strokes might reflect anxiety and frustration, but by the end the stokes would show tranquil peace despite the hardness of life. For once, I was doing an activity that didn't have a "correct" outcome. My perfectionism quickly had to yield to my sometimes imperfectly placed strokes, which brought about more joy and peace than I ever expected. I finally began to embrace my imperfections as unique beauty.

Being in an emotionally and spiritually healthy place, thanks to a couple of years of intentional healing work and professional counseling, I knew exactly what I wanted my first official painting to be. I wanted to paint the words that I couldn't yet formulate.

I entitled the painting "Thriving Survivor." The painting portrayed a daisy with one black petal fallen off. The daisy was set in a peaceful, green field with a rose gold sky.

The soft rose gold sky and lush green grass represent my warm, safe, and loving background that remains to this day. As you have seen, I never wanted for much—love or otherwise. Although I now have my own home, our family acreage represents my truest safe place.

As the flower, flourishing where I was planted was easy despite some growing pains. The bright yellow center of the daisy represents my faith in the Life Giver, the center of my life. The white petals represent the purity culture in which I grew up. Good or bad, right or wrong, correctly perceived or distorted, great emphasis was placed on purity. I don't fault Dad and Mom for giving me a purity ring or framing my purity covenant, because they did so from a place of love and desire to protect me from pain. It was never motivated by archaic views of women, as they held my brothers to the same standards. My parents didn't intend the condemnation that I would eventually feel from these items.

The black petal represents my loss—what was ripped away

from me when I was raped. I didn't know when I would share this part of my story. Even after dealing with the shame, I wanted to wait to share this story until my grandparents were no longer on this depraved earth to spare them the pain of knowing what was done to me. But I couldn't stay silent anymore.

My deeper desire is to reassure other women who have faced similar trauma that it's okay to not be okay, and that there's hope. Psychological damage and PTSD cause many survivors to act and speak illogically and inconsistently for the days, weeks, months, and even years after the trauma.

I'm sure that my parents often worried that I would be taken advantage of by men. After all, disabled women are among the most likely to experience sexual abuse or assault. This is likely why I have a vivid memory of a conversation with Dad at the end of one of our daddy-daughter dates when I was young. "If a guy ever tries to touch you or hurt you, you scream bloody murder and hit him with everything you have. Hit him between the legs and in the face," Dad said in a serious voice. I naively promised I would.

My logical self would have screamed for help as Dad taught me—not whimpered and cried, "No!" until my futile pleading ceased, and I was transformed into an object, mind in a faraway place—seeing my longed-for white wedding disintegrate into ashes in my mind's eye. Again, one day I hope to write a book dissecting the church's emphasis on purity in light of the overwhelming likelihood that Christian women will face sexual abuse, assault, or rape during their lifetimes. Here, I'm merely telling my story to the extent beneficial for showing God's grace in my life.

Every woman's abuse or assault story is hers and hers alone to share or not share to the extent she chooses. Unless seeking legal retribution against her attacker, she need not share any details that she doesn't wish. Although I'm currently choosing and may continue to choose not to publicly divulge the who-what-when-where-how details of my traumatic encounter, I choose to speak on how the rape affected me emotionally and spiritually.

It's a mystery how I felt every physical pain inflicted by my abuser while feeling like a hollow shell. Yet I was still emotionally distraught enough to quietly exclaim "sorry" at each harsh thrust of my abuser. He probably didn't know or care what I was saying at that point, but even in my delirium, I was verbally apologizing to my future love who I'd been waiting for all those years before. When comprehension became more painful still, my mind grasped at lush green grass images of my tranquil childhood.

When my ultimate villain left me bleeding, I was able to pull myself back into my wheelchair and reach my phone. I called Stephanie. Yes, this was another one of those desperate calls that my dear friend received. She was living in Houston, working on her master's at the time. She knew something was very wrong but couldn't make sense of what I told her because I didn't even want to admit what had happened. Essentially, all she knew was that I felt I'd made a terrible mistake, and something had gone wrong with a guy.

You see, it was supposed to be my choice when to give this part of me to another. Because my mind was marred when hopes of how I would make the choice didn't match my broken reality, I blended the two into false memories. I created an alternate reality to survive law school and pass the bar exam. I believed there wasn't enough evidence for a conviction, but my loved ones would want to fight anyway, so I shut them out of my misery. I didn't want a trial, I just wanted to be free, but at the same time stayed enslaved for many months. Humiliated by my weaknesses, I simultaneously tried to construct a reality more bearable—a reality where what was taken from me was strictly physical with no mental or emotional component.

Feeling a twisted bond to my ultimate villain, trying to comprehend that which I should never have needed to comprehend, I believed many untrue things: "It's my fault, because I didn't scream or fight back hard enough like my dad taught me. I have to figure out a way to make it work because no one else will want me now. I'm just a worthless, damaged, and used disabled woman now, and my family would be so ashamed."

As I yearned for my yester-self, I irrationally tried to reconnect with unmarried guys from my small Bible college to remind me of the girl who I used to be while simultaneously starting new unhealthy online relationships in accordance with who I believed I'd become.

Striving to live with a secret of that magnitude only adds to the psychological damage of PTSD. To my closest friends, my actions were totally disjointed. I went from conservative Christian to liberal theist. The little spiritual strength that I had left from the battle wounds of law school vanished. In my mind, I was a theist through and through but didn't wish to argue with my parents, so I kept my struggles to myself. As much as I longed to be an atheist because I didn't want to live in a world where God would allow a disabled woman who had followed Him through the fires of life to be raped, I intellectually couldn't vanish God from existence. I find it ironic that atheists deem themselves intellectuals, because I see the hand of God everywhere. Even when my anger at Him was at an all-time high, looking back over my life, I couldn't deny His existence even during my darkest days.

The problem was that my very life proved God's existence. He had to be a personable God. This debunked many of the other religions that I wanted to believe had the same validity as Christianity. Going one step further, as much as I wasn't His fan, I didn't believe He was a God of chaos. Therefore, He likely desired to reveal Himself to humanity, which led me back to the Bible.

The Bible is one of the only books displaying God as an orderly, personable God. To my chagrin, on a daily basis, my mind took me from my atheist desires to theism to a disgruntled Christian. The fact that I repeatedly returned to my Christian faith didn't mean that I was any less annoyed by peppy and joyful Christians. They made me livid. I'll never be one to share the gospel as "come to Jesus and either your circumstances or your mental health will be instantaneously perfected!"

As you can see from my story, I have been through the fire, and the only hope is that God's ways are higher than mine in light of this fallen world. He doesn't desire pain for His children, but neither does He desire perfectly controlled robots.

Although I continued to operate in a fog as I'd done most of law school, I utterly refused to allow this trauma to stop me from becoming an attorney. I was so close to the finish line—mere months from graduating and taking the bar exam. Even more compelling, I had the job offer from a large firm in my pocket. My only goal was to push my way through the next few months until I started a "new life."

I imagined my new beginning would somehow diminish the horrors of my past. I pictured myself as a strong and skilled attorney who no longer desired romantic relationships. Ultimately, my unresolved emotional and spiritual baggage followed me to my new job. To my horror, the job was just another level of torture similar to the Greek myth where the man was eternally condemned to roll a boulder up a hill. Some of the angst with my job was certainly due to my baggage. However, looking back after years of intense counseling and spiritual healing, it is crystal clear that the job in and of itself was simply awful as well.

Prior to counseling, upon realizing that this job was a never-ending attempt to please unpleasant individuals, I fell even deeper into depression. My saving grace was the church I began attending after taking the bar. My former youth pastor was the preaching pastor at the church campus I attended, which led to a great spiritual revitalization in my damaged soul. I also joined a Bible study for the first time in years. Fellowshipping with a group of young women also led to rebuilding my relationship with God little by little. Heather, my lifelong best friend, was a part of the Bible study, so for the first time since I began law school, we saw each other at least once a week. Her friendship brought much-needed stability to my life, although she didn't yet know of the trauma I'd experienced just a few months prior.

Yet the undealt-with trauma and depression persisted even as my faith became steadier. A mere number of months after becoming an attorney, I began a private relationship with a man whom I was in no way attracted to. My aim—secure marriage to a Christian man whom family liked so I would no longer have to work in such a harsh environment. The relationship itself was private because, unlike me, he had no qualms about being honest that I wasn't his first choice. He simply wanted to keep the option of marrying a "good Christian girl" from a solid family open in case nothing better came along. I genuinely tried to love him, but I would be lying if I said I didn't find a certain amount of comfort in knowing that he would never touch or sexually abuse me. Every time he made a hurtful comment about my attractiveness in light of my cerebral palsy, I found a certain amount of solace in the words because any type of physical intimacy seemed evil to its core.

When the relationship abruptly ended, my depression further deepened. I could only see myself perpetually pushing the boulder of my detested job until I grew old and gray. For the first time in my entire life, I began taking antidepressant medication. The final straw was my multiple suicide attempts the summer after the relationship ended. Anna had agreed to stay with me for a month during the summer to care for me. Even with her constant joyful friendship, I still simply wanted to die and go to heaven where I would be freed from not only physical suffering, but also my emotional pain.

Unbeknownst to anyone else, early in the morning, I would get out of bed and make my way to the pool area of the apartment complex. Plunging into the peaceful waters with my heavy wheelchair seemed a tranquil way to end my life. Truth be told, not only did I long to be in heaven, but I longed to cause the emotionally abusive man pain by broadcasting once and for all that he had driven me to do. I wanted my family to burn with hatred toward him the way I did. My suicidal plans were foiled every time because the gate was always locked—I went too early in the morning. At the end of each failed attempt, I would return to my apartment, crawl back into bed, and await arising to trudge off to my boulder once again.

Then, I had another thought one early morning, throw myself off the bridge into the river behind my apartment complex. My actions in wheeling out to the bridge were among the most selfish of my entire life—premeditated, not panic-induced. I sat overlooking the river for a long time. People passed me on the bike trail. Some asked if I was okay—probably thrown off by the sight of a wheelchair-bound young woman with messy hair, wearing a nightgown. I stayed out too long because, to Anna's horror, I wasn't in my bed when she went to help me get ready for the workday.

She called my cell phone multiple times. I finally answered. I told her where I was.

She came crying to get me and bring me back to safety. She was also on the phone with Mom after I told her where I was—I remember repeatedly saying, "Don't make me go to work today."

I cringe to think of what I put Anna, Mom, and Dad, and my other loved ones through. It wasn't fair to cause them so much pain and worry. Jamison eventually had to console Mom by telling her, "If Janae takes her life, it will not be your fault." Stephanie received yet another desperate phone call. So did my first roommate, Amber. Both communicated concerns to Mom.

The result: I returned to work the next day, but my cousin took me to the doctor to get antidepressants. I felt comfort that she was the one who went with me, knowing that she had her own emotional turmoil. I must have answered the doctor's questions pretty dramatically because he prescribed double the dose I actually needed. When Anna woke me up the next morning, my pupils were dilated, I was sweaty, dizzy, and largely unable to communicate. Mom was out of town, so Grandma came and cared for me for the day until Anna returned from her other job. Grandma caring for me also brought great comfort, as I was able to return to a state of semi-childhood.

Once we obtained the correct dosage, the medication helped greatly. I also went to a few counseling sessions. Yet I eventually stopped going because the counselor couldn't see past my disability to my other emotional issues. At this time, I'd still expressly told no one of my rape. The counselor wasn't able to pick up on it, even though I felt I gave multiple clues, hoping she would prod for more answers.

My friend Erica also stayed with me during the second part of the summer when Anna went on a mission trip to Africa. Erica, a dear and close friend from my Bible college days, brought so much healing to my life. I truly needed her to get my life back on track and keep living for the Lord. Our summer days together were some of my favorites, but eventually, she had to return to Wisconsin and begin teaching another school year.

By the time Erica left, I was functioning normally again. I lived as normally as possible for the next year. Yet I still developed unhealthy relationships with men online. Recently, my friend Dana said that trauma victims frequently seek out ways to relive their trauma. Never having heard this fact before, everything about that time period finally made sense to me. That is exactly what I was doing in some way. No, I didn't have a series of one-night stands, but I definitely had a series of relationships where men would either emotionally or physically hurt me.

My only public relationship ever was the most utterly ridiculous relationship of my life. Still, although completely unattracted to this man, I was again able to disconnect myself from my physical being, watching the relationship unfold as if a movie that I was merely viewing. I went through the motions, said the words, and posted the pictures, merely to prove that I was, in fact, lovable. Crumbling after barely a month, the relationship ultimately failed because he had no qualities that I desired other than being a Christian man who desired me.

Ending the relationship was the first healthy relationship choice I'd made in years. This was probably largely due to my finally participating in regular, weekly counseling with a counselor who finally "got me." Had I not finally broken down and told Mom and Dad of the rape, I would have not been in counseling. Another breakdown that contributed to me being in counseling was my final attempt to physically harm myself. It occurred in my office just weeks after telling Mom, Dad, and my closest friends about the rape.

At the time, Anna was working as my office assistant but was planning to return to school in the next few months. We were blindsided by yet another meeting by my superiors telling me that I wasn't measuring up to the firm's standards. At that point, I simply wanted my parents to promise to support me if I quit this oppressive job. I returned to my private office, and while Anna was in the bathroom, I resorted to cutting my wrists with scissors. Again, so extremely unfair to make Anna handle my mental instability on her own. Yet in my own twisted mind, this was the only way to get out of my work entrapment.

Initially, I was disappointed that all my parents did was pay for counseling. Looking back now, I see that God was actually paving the way for me to leave my job. Yet He wanted me to do it from a place of confidence and power, not weakness and defeat. He wanted me to become mentally healthy enough to use my God-given gifts and talents to plan my next steps. Counseling gave me the tools I needed to think correctly about my life. I dealt with my rape. I dealt with the part I played in my emotionally abusive relationship. Not only did we touch on disability issues, but also, I dealt head-on with the perfectionism that so crippled me into feeling like a failure.

More office turmoil at the firm led to me working from home. Cunning enough to present my relocation as most beneficial to me, the firm managed to save face. Initially, I was disappointed to work from home. Yet as I talked through the situation with my counselor, I came to realize that working from home was a blessing. Not only did eliminate the need for transportation by caregivers to and from the office, but also, I was further distanced from the less-than-pleasant work environment. I could write documents, get paid, and not have to worry about surprise confrontations with supervisors possessing very limited compassion.

But the ultimate blessing was that sheer desperation led me to hire a woman who, unbeknownst to me, would become my most valuable assistant to date. You've already met her in chapter one of this book. Her name is Sharalee. I didn't even know her name when I went to message her about considering working for me. Oddly enough, a few years prior, my cousin recommended that I ask Sharalee to be my work assistant. At the time, I worried that her peppy personality would cause us not to get along. Further, her status as a pastor's wife worried me. Would she judge me? God's timing is perfect because had I asked her a few years earlier, we would have had to navigate her pregnancies and maternity leaves. In God's great timing, I asked her at a time when she was ready to work outside the home.

Sharalee's personality and authenticity greatly helped my depression. Over the first months we worked together, we challenged each other in our faith and battles against depression and anxiety. Being a few years older than I, she was able to add an additional component of wisdom to evaluating my job situation. Yet she still saw firsthand how much I lacked any career enjoyment.

When I began this book, the basic message was how to never give up. You see, although I overcame so many emotional and spiritual hurdles when I began writing this book, I was still working at the firm. With the unwavering support of family and friends, I was joyfully living even when life hurt. I was waiting for God to lead me to a more fulfilling career. Thankfully, He used physical pain and fatigue to compel me to cut my hours a few years prior. With more free time and less painful delirium, I began to dream of a writing career. Taking a step of faith, I wrote over half of this book in one weekend with the help of Becca.

I felt I would never struggle with suicidal ideations again. A few short weeks after writing the majority of this book, I faced another conflict at work. An overwhelmingly familiar feeling washed over me like a chill. "God, you can't possibly want me to keep working here! The only time I have suicidal thoughts is when these people make me feel that I'll never measure up and that I should be thankful I have any job at all."

Phone calls with loved ones, a few emergency counseling

sessions, and many tears later, I felt I finally had a plan that justified resigning my position at the firm. Although dealing with many depressive thoughts, unlike all the other times I wasn't crippled into hopelessness. As I sought God, He paved the way for me to resign.

Complete surrender to God is so sweet. I stopped fighting against my physical limitations and pain. I stopped trying to prove to everyone that I was just as good. Finally, I stopped fighting my cerebral palsy and embraced it fully as God's good plan in my life. Looking up to heaven with upturned palms, I said, "God, you made me. You know me. I'm done trying to prove myself to them. Do what you will with my life."

Since the day I resigned for disability-related reasons, I have hadn't one ounce of regret. Shoots of sporadic anger at the firm make it clear that I'm still in the process of forgiveness, but I pray that I'll achieve this someday. In the meantime, I find overwhelming joy and peace awaiting me each day when I awake.

As I work in my private law practice, according to my varying physical stamina, I praise God for the intellect that allows me to work as much as I'm able. As I live my life in dependence upon my faithful caregivers, I find peace and joy in living life with them by my side. We paint. We clean the house. We do laundry. We shop. We order takeout. At random moments during all of these activities, I'm overwhelmed by the grace of God who brought me out of my dark days. Even as I play and laugh with my nieces and nephews, sometimes my eyes mist over when I think of how these moments used to be overshadowed by internal depression and external oppression. Fridays with Mom are no less blissful than in my dark days because now we merely enjoy each other's company rather than her having to try so hard to lift my spirits.

But for my change in career, life's circumstances aren't much different than during my darkest days. My past is still there.

My disability still hinders every activity in my life. I'm still romantically alone. I still worry about caregivers and assistants moving on and leaving me. And, in all honesty, some days I still battle depression and anxiety. The difference is that these are the things I have resolved to joyfully fight until the blessed day when I'm face-to-face with Christ. I count myself truly blessed beyond what I deserve because I have changed the unpleasant aspects of my life that God allowed, and have been graced with unexplainable joy in not only my brightest days, but also my darkest days.

Future Hope

As you read the pages of my story, I hope you experienced many emotions—love, laughter, and hope, but also betrayal, sorrow, and darkness. But isn't this an accurate picture of all of our lives? Surely all of us could write a similar story, detailing our victories and defeats, joys and devastations, and laughter and pains.

Even as I sit here dictating the final words of this book to my faithful assistant, Becca, I'm faced with many uncertainties of life. Will my business continue to succeed? What happens if I lose my most valuable assistants? Will I ever know the true love of a man in the romantic sense? Most terrifyingly, when will my parents die, and who will be my first call when they do?

If left to our own devices, we can all drive ourselves nearly insane with questions of uncertainty. So, after all we have been through thus far in our lives, how do we deal with the pain of the unknown? The answer is simple, but complex—faith in our Creator. We look back, not with rose-colored glasses, but with full awareness of the pain and suffering we have been through. But, even amidst the carnage of our broken lives, if we truly pause and ponder, we can also see the breathtaking glimmers of the golden thread of grace, running through each painful or blissful moment.

Seeing this thread running through my path with its golden rays even in the most painful times, gives me hope for the future. Today, even as I sit in the peaceful waters of my present life, I'm not oblivious to the fact that new storms will arise in the future, whether distant or immediate. I'm well aware that new circumstances will cause new physical and emotional damage. I'll once again have to burrow down deep to weather the harsh winds, but now with a growing awareness of Jesus' presence.

Yet as my past shines bright with moments of grace, and my eyes look towards the heavens for strength, I can face my unknown future with confidence and dignity. Even when clouds obstruct my view of glimmering moments of grace, my mind remains confident that they exist. As I look toward eternity, the ultimate glowing of grace for me, a fallen, broken human in need of redemption by an unconditionally loving Savior.

Printed in Great Britain
by Amazon